A CHRISTIAN'S RESPONSE TO ISLAM

JAMES L. GARLOW

Compliments of

Dr. James Garlow
Senior Pastor
Skyline Wesleyan Church

and

Sunday School
& Discipleship

Dr. Ray E. Barnwell

RIVER
OAK
PUBLISHING

2nd Printing

A Christian's Response to Islam
ISBN 1-58919-936-7
46-628-00000
Copyright © 2002 by Jim Garlow

Published by RiverOak Publishing
P.O. Box 700143
Tulsa, Oklahoma 74170-0143

TABLE OF CONTENTS

DEDICATED TO THOSE CHRISTIANS WHO

Have lost their lives due to Muslim militancy,

Are, or have been, the victims of
Muslim persecution, and

Are currently imprisoned for their faith
in Muslim countries.

FOREWORD

This was never intended to be a book. It began simply as a personal letter to a pastor friend of mine who had e-mailed me, telling me that his congregation had invited Muslims to their church following the September 11, 2001, terrorist attack on America. According to my friend's message, his congregation stood and applauded for the Muslims. I e-mailed him my response. After I sent it, I realized that it was a type of "position paper," so I e-mailed it to several more friends. I never could have anticipated what occurred next.

Within an hour I began hearing from people as far away as Paris, France. Almost everyone indicated they were forwarding it to their entire e-mail address lists. People asked if they could copy it, print it, post it on Web sites, read it over radio stations. Some pastors read the entire twelve-page, double-column letter to their congregations. Simply stated, the "letter" quickly went "far and wide."

During the next few days, more than seven hundred personally written e-mails came to me (I read every one—carefully), 97 percent thanking me for what I had written. I began to see a pattern in the responses. Almost all were positive ("I never knew this. Thank you for this."). A few were negative or, at least, challenging. ("How dare you suggest that the Koran has violent passages? How dare you criticize Muslims? They worship the same God we do." "Islam is a religion of peace!") Most intriguing were the many comments from those who have worked in Muslim nations or who were formerly

Muslim. By far the most encouraging were the statements that indicated my e-mail had encouraged a greater passion for Christ. ("Your letter helped me be more bold for Jesus.") Along with the e-mails came vigorous chat-room discussions on the topic and hundreds of private conversations.

Because of the widespread distribution of the letter, I also had the privilege of hearing from persons who were once Muslim (MBBs as they are called: Muslim Background Believers) and have come to embrace Jesus as the resurrected Son of God. I was able to spend time with these new friends, asking them about Islam, what it was like being Muslim, how they came to leave Islam, and then hearing accounts of—in some cases—the attempts on their lives due to their Christian conversions.

In past years, I had received several graduate degrees on the history of Christianity. Islam would enter the "story line" but only tangentially. After September 11, 2001, I decided to spend study time exclusively dedicated to understanding Islam better—reading, studying, interviewing—spending nearly one thousand hours in the four months following the New York City/Washington, D.C. attacks. I chose to read not only Christian and Jewish writings but Islamic sources as well. In order to understand what is happening in contemporary, present-day Islam country by country, I took a course on the current trends of various national Muslim communities.

As a result of the whirlwind created by one simple e-mail letter, this book came to be. And it has one agenda: to increase love and boldness for Christ with the result that we more effectively share Him with all (including Muslims), rather than simply "blending in" with our multireligious culture.

Before you read the following pages, I need to give clarification and make a disclaimer. This is not primarily a book about Islam. This is a Christian's response to Islam. There are many great books available on Muslims and Islam. This small book is looking at one issue only.

Furthermore, the book is not titled *The Christian Response,* which would suggest that I am speaking for all Christians. I am not. It is titled *A Christian's Response,* that is, one Christian's response—specifically mine.

I am not trying to appease our multicultural generation in this work. This is a *Christian* response. I am a follower of Jesus Christ. If you are not a follower of Jesus Christ, you may disagree with what I have to say. But it needs to be noted that I am responding as a follower of Jesus. I take seriously Jesus' claim to be "the way, the truth, and the life" and that no one goes to the Father except through Him. (See John 14:6.) A Christian, as I understand the term, embraces the notion that Jesus is the only way of salvation.

And finally, this book is *for* Christians, written *to* Christians, *by* a Christian. This book is not written to Muslims. If it were, I would have written it very differently. I recognize that Muslims may pick it up and read it, but it was designed for Christians, specifically to challenge Christians.

CHAPTER ONE

A DIFFERENT WORLD

September 11, 2001, changed our lives forever. On that day, nineteen Islamic fundamentalists hijacked four passenger jets and flew two of them directly into both World Trade Center towers in New York City and one into the Pentagon in Washington, D.C. The fourth plane, allegedly headed for either the United States Capitol or the White House, crashed into a field in rural Pennsylvania. The devastation and loss of life was incredible. This was not just a major news story. Our world changed forever on that day. The "post-9-11" world is much different than the "pre-9-11" world.

In a speech before the U.S. House of Representatives Government Reform Committee on September 20, 2001, former Israeli Prime Minister Benjamin Netanyahu soberly stated, "What is at stake is nothing less than the survival of our civilization. There may be some who would have thought a week ago that to talk in these apocalyptic terms . . . was to engage in reckless exaggeration. No longer . . . We are all targets."[1]

One of the most visible changes in the "post-9-11" world is the way we view Muslims and the religion of Islam. Most Americans had no idea that Islam was the fastest growing religion in the world (percentagewise), including in America. But "9-11" changed all that. And that is why I had to write this book.

NEW WORDS

Within days after September 11, new words entered our conversational vocabulary. "Bioterrorism," "anthrax," and "Taliban" were only a few that we began to hear and read many times a day. But the one word that introduced itself most forcefully into the American vocabulary was "Islam," along with its accompanying term "Muslim." Most of us have heard these terms used more times in the days following the terrorist attack than at any other time in our lives.

Amazingly, Americans emerged from September 11 with a far more *favorable* view of Islam. The rush to embrace Islam academically is demonstrated by the fact that prior to September 11, a survey of some nine hundred university religion and theology departments by the Lilly Endowment showed that a third of them offered no courses on Islam. Now universities are in a bidding war for Islamic experts; for the next semester most scheduled courses on Islam are oversubscribed.

ISLAMIC GROWTH

Many individuals were not aware of the prevalence of Muslims in America and around the globe until after September 11. Here are some shocking statistics:

* Some estimate as high as 1.4 *billion* Muslims in the world, which equates to nearly 1 out of every 4 people (a more conservative estimate places it at 1 out of every 5 persons, with a total of 1.2 billion Muslims).

* There are as many as 7 million Muslims in the United States;

* 307 million Muslims in Africa;

* 778 million Muslims in Asia;

* 32 million Muslims in Europe; and

* 1.4 million Muslims in Latin America.

* Although India is predominantly Hindu, there are 100 million Muslims in that country as well.

* There are as many Muslims in Indonesia (nearly 150 million) as there are Arab Muslims in the central Middle East.

* Islam is the second largest religious group in the United States, behind Christianity and likely ahead of Judaism.

* Islam is the second largest religion in Europe behind Christianity.

* Muslims are in the majority in forty-five African and Asian countries.

* The global birthrate after the year 2055 will be at least 50 percent Muslim, according to the United Nations.[2]

* In terms of impacting the world, Harvard professor Samuel Huntingdon has compared the "Islamic Resurgence" in the late twentieth century to that of the Protestant Reformation in the late sixteenth century.

* Social revolution occurs through youth, and in Muslim countries, the number of youth between 15 and 24 years of age has exceeded 20 percent of the population.[3]

* Almost half of the 300 million Arabs are under the age of 15.

* There are only 2-3 Christian missionaries for every 1 million Muslims.[4]

* The number of mosques in the United States has increased 25 percent in the last five years.[5]

With all of this growth worldwide, we need to ask some vital questions, starting with: *What is Islam? Who are the Muslims?* When former Israeli Prime Minister Benjamin Netanyahu stated on September 24, 2001, on Fox News' *Hannity and Colmes* show that "this new virulent stream of militant Islam . . . wants to reverse a thousand years of history," what did he mean? When President George W. Bush stated repeatedly that Islam is a religion of peace, what did he mean? And, if it is a religion of peace, why are Muslims attacking our country? How are we to understand the seeming "love affair" with Islam among scholars, students, some church attenders, and Americans in general?

Let's bring the questions a little closer to home:

* Do Muslims worship the same God I do (as a Christian)?

* And if they worship the same God, then why should I attempt to evangelize them?

* Out of respect for other religions, should I avoid mentioning Christ so that I can establish a type of "common denominator" ("God," in general) with other religions such as Islam?

* Or should I view them as persons who are not prepared to enter into eternity (since they do not know Christ)?

* In the midst of terrorist attacks on the United States, why all this talk about Israel? About Palestine? And even about Ishmael and Isaac?

* What do those countries and persons have to do with terrorists attacking America?

* Does my Bible shed light on this controversy?

Here is one more question—a good place for us to end the questions and begin to explore the answers:

* Does all of this really matter? Why can't we just "live and let live"?

It is important for contemporary believers to "understand the times." First Chronicles 12:32 states that the descendants of Issachar discerned the times and knew what Israel ought to do. As followers of Christ, it is imperative that we, too, discern the times—and that we know what we, the Church, ought to do.

NEEDED DISCERNMENT

Spiritually speaking, we are "citizens of Jerusalem" (followers of Christ). But we also "live in Babylon" (a culture that is typically against Christian values). Tragically, we have embraced much "Babylonian" (un-Christian) thinking. What is worse is that we don't even know it. Many followers of Christ today embrace many "cultural myths" which they believe to be true without realizing that they are actually antibiblical. They have embraced positions and views that are precisely the opposite of what the Bible proclaims as truth. We have assumed that popular American "myths" are "Christian" when, in reality, they oppose what the Bible actually teaches. It is my hope that we will regain a clear understanding of scriptural teaching regarding our thoughts and actions in today's culture.

Now, let's take a look at Islam and find out what it means to be a follower of Christ—specifically regarding how to respond to Islam.

CHAPTER TWO

ISHMAEL AND ISAAC—
TWO BROTHERS WHO CHANGED HISTORY

This book is a focused look at my response, as a
Christian, to Islam. However, in order for us to understand
the events you see portrayed on the news each day, we need
to take a brief look at the story of the Jews (the descendants
of Isaac) and follow that (in the next chapter) with the story
of the Muslims (some of whom are descendants of Ishmael).

The answers to the questions you may have been asking
since the September 11, 2001, terrorist attacks are rooted in
events that happened long ago. As with so many other subjects, we must know where we have been before we can
really know where we are going. I will try to make this
"walk" through history as painless and as entertaining as I
possibly can. Do not become discouraged by seeing some
words that are new to you. Just try to get an overview of the
story. If you will read this chapter and the next, much of
what you read in the newspaper will suddenly make sense.
Here we go.

AN UNLIKELY BIRTH

In the land of Chaldea, in the city of Ur, there lived a
man called Abram. In approximately 2000 B.C., Abram
received a message from Jehovah God telling him to leave
the land of his ancestors and go to a land God would show

him. So Abram left Ur with his wife, Sarai. They eventually arrived in the land of Canaan, which today is called Israel.

Abram and Sarai settled in the land of Canaan. They fought battles, increased their wealth, and rescued their nephew Lot from kings who raided his city. But Abram felt unfulfilled—he had no son to carry on his name. God came to Abram once again.

Then the LORD took Abram outside and said, "Look at the sky and see if you can count the stars. That's how many descendants you will have" (Genesis 15:5 CEV). God's promise to Abram was for a son that would be the beginning of a lineage God would bless through the ages. When Abram repeated this conversation to his wife, she did not see how God could do it. After all, she and Abram were quite old—and they had never been able to conceive children. So Sarai came up with a plan to "help" God, one that was common in the Ancient Near East: Abram would sleep with her maid, Hagar. Hagar did become pregnant, and she gave Abram a son he named Ishmael. But this was not the son God promised. A few years later, God visited Abram yet again. He changed Abram's name to Abraham and Sarai's name to Sarah. And then a miracle occurred: Sarah, at age ninety, found herself to be with child. She gave birth to Isaac, the son God had promised would be the first of many descendants.

I have told this story for this reason: The offspring of Abraham is the focal point of the current conflict. The ongoing struggle in the Middle East is a direct result of the animosity between the descendants of Ishmael and Isaac. While there is no record of Ishmael and Isaac ever fighting each other, Genesis does record God's prophecy regarding Ishmael: *He will be against everyone, and everyone will be against him* (Genesis 16:12 TEV). Today's struggle is between those who call themselves the descendants of Ishmael and those who call themselves descendants of Isaac. The intense struggle in Israel and the surrounding Arab nations can only be understood historically as a struggle between the descendants of two brothers who lived four thousand years ago: Ishmael (modern-day Arabs) and Isaac (the Jews).

(There is a dispute among some scholars as to whether or not many Arabs are actually descendants of Ishmael. Some even question whether some of the Jews immigrating to Israel are actually descendants of Isaac. However, the issue, at this point, is irrelevant. Arabs *perceive* themselves to be Ishmael's descendants. Ishmael's descendants, who are listed in Genesis 25:16-18, settled in North Arabia. Approximately 300 million of the world's 1.4 billion Muslims are Arabs. Jews *perceive* themselves to be descendants of Isaac. *Perception* is sometimes stronger than any reality. For our purposes, we will refer to Arabs as Ishmael's offspring and Jews as Isaac's offspring.)

Let me remind you that this story is not just about Ishmael and Isaac. This is not simply about *their past*—it is about *your future.* And specifically, it is not only their story—it is *your* story.

ISHMAEL

As Isaac and Ishmael grew, Sarah became jealous of Ishmael. She told Abraham to send the boy of her maid away. This saddened Abraham; after all, Ishmael was his son. But God comforted Abraham. He promised to care for Ishmael and his mother but again told Abraham that it was to be through Isaac that the descendants as numerous as the stars would come.

The Bible tells us much about Ishmael. God promises that although Abraham's firstborn is not the promised child, He will bless Ishmael. Ishmael was a warrior, a skilled archer (Genesis 21:20). Ishmael is also described as being like "a wild donkey" (Genesis 16:12). The Bible states that Ishmael will have so many descendants that they can't be counted (Genesis 16:10). God promised that he would make a great nation from Ishmael (Genesis 21:18). In fact, the concern of God for the boy Ishmael is one of the most tender passages in the Bible (Genesis 21:17-20). But there are ominous passages as well: He will settle east of Egypt and he will be settled in defiance of all their relatives *and he will live in hostility toward all his brothers* (Genesis 16:12).

ABRAHAM, ISAAC, JACOB, JOSEPH

In approximately 2000 B.C., Abraham fathered Isaac; Isaac was father to Jacob; Jacob became father to Joseph. These four remarkable generations span much of the book of Genesis. By the end of Genesis, the Israelites are in Egypt, at first as guests of their political leader and relative Joseph. Later, however, they are held against their wills, held by an unsympathetic Pharaoh. We won't cover the stories of their lives, not because they are unimportant but because their stories are often told and well known. But their lives lay the foundation for understanding today's Israeli-Arab conflict.

By the time of Joseph, the descendants of Abraham were so numerous they were no longer simply a family; they had become a people. The Egyptians, who held them against their will, greatly feared them.

MOSES AND JOSHUA

Finally, after years of bondage in slavery, Moses led the Israelites (at that time anywhere from 600,000 to 2 million in number) out of Egypt in approximately 1500 B.C. The Israelites took a most circuitous route, which included four decades of "wandering" with an entire generation dying in the Sinai desert.

And although Moses successfully led the Israelites *out* of Egypt, it was Joshua who led them *in*—to the land God had promised them. Before Moses died at Mount Nebo on the east side of the Jordan River he saw a beautiful sight. He looked across the Jordan River, and saw the land that his relatives would receive. But he never entered in. Joshua took them in.

JUDGES AND KINGS

Once in their new homeland, they needed some type of governmental structure. They formed a loose coalition of tribes that were noncentralized and somewhat democratic. Whenever they were threatened by a strong foe, God raised up a "judge." The judge would lead the people in overcoming their foe. The Book of Judges from the Old Testament is a listing of about a dozen men and one woman, who, raised up by God, helped govern Israel.

In approximately 1000 B.C., the Israelites began to say, "Everybody else has a king. We want a king." God didn't want them to have a king, but they insisted. So God acquiesced and allowed them to have a king, actually three kings, in succession: Saul, David, then Solomon.

CIVIL WAR: NORTH VS. SOUTH

In approximately 900 B.C., Israel split "north" and "south," launching a civil war. The land south of Jerusalem took the name "Judah" and became the Southern Kingdom. The Northern Kingdom kept the name "Israel" (which is admittedly confusing due to the fact that throughout history, the entire area—both north and south—was also called Israel). The Northern Kingdom included all the area around the Sea of Galilee.

The Northern Kingdom, Israel, had 19 wicked kings over the next few hundred years. Eventually, Assyria conquered Israel and carried them away approximately seven hundred years before Christ. Numerous prophets (preachers) warned them that this was going to happen: Elijah, Elisha, Jonah, Amos and Hosea. These northerners disappeared from the "radar screen" of history.

The Southern Kingdom existed from approximately 900 B.C. to 600 B.C. During that time, 20 kings—8 who had integrity, or at least began their reign that way, and 12 who were blatantly wicked—ruled Judah. Approximately 600 B.C., the Babylonian (present-day Iraq) armies overtook Judah and exiled the inhabitants. Isaiah, Jeremiah, Joel, Obadiah, Micah, Nahum, Habakkuk, and Zephaniah were some of the prophets who had warned them concerning what was going to happen. They tried to warn the Israelis to repent so that destruction would not come to them.

EXILE AND RETURN

Israel did not repent, and in 600 B.C. they were taken away and held as captives for approximately seventy years. (It is important to note that Israel would not be a sovereign nation from 600 B.C. until it was established as a nation in modern times in 1948. Israel would be dominated and ruled by outside forces almost continually for two thousand years.)

After seventy years in Babylon, they began in making their way back to Israel in several "waves," trying to rebuild what was there—especially reconstructing the Temple. The first "return" occurred in approximately 540 B.C. Another group came in approximately 460 B.C. And another group returned to Israel in 440 B.C. Haggai, Zechariah, and Malachi wrote their prophecies during this postexilic time.

NATIONS: COME AND GO

The Assyrians, who captured the Northern Kingdom, did not last long as a superpower. The Babylonians who had conquered the Southern Kingdom, were soon overpowered by the Persians (approximately 500 B.C.), who were eventually overpowered by the Greeks (approximately 400 B.C.), who were finally defeated by the Romans (approximately 100 B.C.) who had had a five hundred-year tenure, when Rome was sacked in approximately A.D. 400.

The Roman Empire was the ruling power over the Jews—and much of the rest of the world at that time—when Jesus was born in Bethlehem. It was the Roman army that crushed a Jewish revolt by destroying Jerusalem in A.D. 70. And it was under Roman rule that the Christian Church was born.

During its first five centuries, Christianity grew rapidly, reaching far beyond Israel. It became the official religion of the entire Roman Empire in A.D. 380. The hunger for the Gospel of Christ was pronounced, especially among Roman soldiers who carried the "good news" across the empire. The Gospel was equally well received by the enormous slave population. It spread like wildfire. It could not be stopped. Or could it? In the 600s, Christianity met one of its greatest opponents: Islam.

We will look at the "Ishmael" portion of this story in the next chapter. For now, we are still concerned with the descendants—both natural and spiritual—of Isaac. But it is at this point in our historical overview that these two half brothers, the two sons of Abraham, collide. And that collision occurs in the heart of Israel: Jerusalem.

Jerusalem is mentioned seven hundred times in the Bible. It is not mentioned in the Koran. King David established this Jewish capitol more than three thousand years ago. Through his kingship it gained prominence. Mohammed was never in Jerusalem, except in a vague "dream" referenced in the Koran. Early Muslims were instructed to pray towards Jerusalem, later towards Mecca. But Jerusalem remains very much in the center of the Jewish-Muslim conflict.

In A.D. 650, Arab Muslim armies took control of Israel. For the next 450 years, from approximately A.D. 650 to A.D. 1100, Muslim Arabs dominated Israel. In approximately A.D. 1100, Pope Urban II called for armies to retake the Holy Lands in the name of Christianity. His speeches inspired armies. The eight military campaigns between 1100 and 1300 were known as the Crusades. The Crusaders made their way to Israel and successfully overthrew the Muslims and controlled parts of Israel for approximately 150 years.

Were these Crusaders truly "Christian"? Hardly! As they made their way across Europe and part of Asia, they pillaged, destroyed, raped, and burned. Many of these soldiers were so-called "second sons," without the promise of land to inherit. They answered the call to battle in exchange for the promise of land grants. These were not missionaries—they were mercenaries. Their actions in no way represented the cause of Christ.

As the Crusaders made their way down to the Holy Land, they went through both Christian and Muslim villages. They were "equal-opportunity offenders." They burned and obliterated villages. They raped the women. They stole what they could. And when American President George W. Bush, in September of 2001, accidentally used the word "crusade" in conversation, it sent shock waves across the Muslim world. Because of the events of September 11, even the Billy Graham Evangelistic Association no longer calls their evangelistic stadium events "crusades."

In 1099, Crusaders, in the name of Jesus, harmed many Muslims. You and I may have no interest in atrocities committed so long ago. But the Muslims remember! Their children are taught in Islamic schools that these were Christians who committed these horrible acts of violence. Muslim children can recite the dates of the Crusades, and they can tell you the stories of what happened to their people. Inaccurate as it may be, in the mind of a Muslim, today's Christian is no different than the soldiers who marched in the Crusades.

After being controlled by Rome, Arab Muslims, and European Crusaders, Jerusalem fell to Egyptian control in A.D. 1250. The Egyptian Mamluk warriors were some of the most advanced military forces in the world. For the next 250 years, the Egyptians occupied Israel, using Islamic soldiers.

In approximately A.D. 1500, the Turks overthrew the Egyptians. And then for the next 400 years—from 1500-1900, the Ottoman Turks, from the area in and around present-day Turkey, controlled Jerusalem. Finally in 1917, during World War I, the British assumed control of Israel.

But Palestine, as Israel was then called, was very difficult to manage. Due to severe conflicts, the British decided to divide the land between the Palestinians (Arabs—Ishmael's descendants) and the Israelis (Jews—Isaac's descendants). The British expected the Israelis and Palestinians to stay on their sides of the established border. But it didn't work that way. The Arabs rioted in 1920 and in 1929. From 1936 to 1939, an intense three-year struggle took place. Succinctly stated, the Palestinians were unwilling to share *any* land with Israel.

Following the end of World War II, the United Nations came up with their version of how to divide the country. The Palestinians rejected it. Patience was running short. The United Nations said in effect, "This is the line. This is the law. Follow it." The British gladly left. And the two nations got along happily ever after? Not exactly. Israel insisted upon and was granted status as an independent nation on May 14, 1948.

ISRAEL—AND THE PALESTINIANS

That was good news for the Jewish people around the world. They finally had a land to call their own. But there was bad news as well. For one thing, the Arab people (known as Palestinians) who had been living there were largely displaced. Seven hundred and fifty thousand left the area in 1948. Also, Jerusalem was a divided city, divided into four quarters—Muslim, Jewish, Armenian, and Christian. Travel from one area to another was difficult. And, thus, the fight continues to this day.

The Arab League of Nations consists of twenty-two countries. These countries wrap around several sides of present-day Israel. Some of these nations have a common agenda:

the elimination of the nation of Israel. And Israel fights back. The numbers are lopsided: Approximately 300 million Arab Muslims surrounding 5 million Jews. The Arabs control 99.9 percent of the Middle East lands. Israel represents one-tenth of 1 percent of the landmass. But God declared the Jews to be His people, and He continues to be with them in their struggles. Against all odds, Israel remains a sovereign nation.

ISRAELIS—GOD'S PEOPLE?

There is disagreement among theologians as to whether or not God's blessing is still on Israel today. Some theologians take the position that God is no longer "contractually" bound to a piece of real estate called Israel. They continue, saying that Paul, in Romans 2 and 3, "redefined" what it means to be a Jew—one who is circumcised inwardly (of the Spirit of God) and not simply outwardly (being a Jew, ethnically). They contend that what "Israel" was in the Old Testament, the "Church" is in the New Testament. They believe God's favor and blessing is not with Israel and the Jews anymore, but with the Church of Jesus Christ. Refuting that position, another group responds, "No, God made His covenant with Israel; it is forever; and even though Israel rejected Jesus as the Messiah, God is committed to honoring Israel." Thus the two sides continue to argue.

Which side is right? Clearly God's favor is on the Church of Jesus Christ. But, at the same time, there is profound evidence of God's protection on that portion of real estate called Israel. I do not claim to have all the answers on this debate. In fact, I have more questions than I do answers. But I am thankful that America has stood with Israel, helping it survive the many attacks against it. Israel is not perfect. Her record has blemishes. She has, at times, abused the Palestinians, just as Palestinians have abused Israelis. And God promised to love Ishmael (ancestor of the Arabs) too. There does, however, seem to be some clear evidence that God has a special place in His heart for the Jewish people and for Israel. It concerns me deeply when people say that the reason for the terrorist attack on September 11 is because of our support of Israel, thus we should stop supporting them. Israel is not the cause. No, the terrorist attack was because of hatred in the hearts of people.

And not supporting Israel would create far more problems for America than she currently has. In the Bible, God promised this nation His protection and warned of harmful consequences to any nation that moves against Israel: *Those who are angry with you will know the shame of defeat. Those who fight against you will die and will disappear from the earth* (Isaiah 41:11-12 TEV). Later in Isaiah, God repeats His promise: *Whoever attacks you, does it without my consent; whoever fights against you will fall. . . . No weapon will be able to hurt you; you will have an answer for all who accuse you. I will defend my servants and give them victory* (Isaiah 54:15,17 TEV). American Christians need to be aware of God's heart when they hear calls to abandon support for the nation of Israel.

That said, we have briefly covered a history of "Isaac's People"—the Jews. Let us now turn our attention to those who claim Ishmael as their father: the followers of Islam and the prophet Mohammed.

CHAPTER THREE

MOHAMMED AND THE MUSLIMS

Who was the founder of this enormous global movement
called Islam? What kind of a life could have inspired the
nearly one and a half billion people who currently follow his
teachings? His name was Mohammed. In this chapter, we
will walk quickly through Mohammed's life as well as
through fourteen hundred years of Islamic history. I have
tried to make it as brief and understandable as possible.
Warning: Many of the words towards the end of this chapter
will seem very strange to us. But, as I said in the previous
chapter, don't become preoccupied with the difficult terms
and potentially confusing dates. Instead, focus on the
"overview" of the story. If you do that—as you hopefully did
with the last chapter—the daily news broadcasts will make
so much more sense.

EARLIEST YEARS

Mohammed was born in A.D. 570 in Mecca, which is part
of present-day Saudi Arabia. For two years he was nursed
by a Bedouin woman named Halima, a common practice at
the time, in order to keep the child in the healthy desert air.
At the age of two, Mohammed's mother, Amina, was so
impressed with the child's healthy appearance that she
asked Halima to take Mohammed back to the desert for
another two years. At age four, Amina was much less
impressed with the health of her son. He suffered from what

may have been epileptic fits, which caused Halima to think that Mohammed was demon possessed. Mohammed, now five, went back to live with his mother. When Amina died, Mohammed's grandfather raised him for the next two years until he died at age eighty. At age twelve, Mohammed was moved to the home of a wealthy uncle, who in turn passed Mohammed on to a poor uncle. As was normal for Arabian youth, he cared for sheep and goats in the hills and valleys surrounding Mecca.

FIRST MARRIAGE

At age twenty-five, Mohammed went to work for a wealthy widow, a forty-year-old merchant named Khadija. Soon after, Mohammed married Khadija, who had been married twice before. She bore him two sons, both of whom died in infancy, and four daughters.

EARLIEST ISLAM

Mohammed grew up in the Quraysh tribe in Mecca. The Quraysh worshiped in the Ka'bah, a 40' x 40' building which housed at least 360 idols and a sacred black stone, a type of "good luck charm." Mohammed later rejected the polytheism (worship of many gods) of the Ka'bah and embraced monotheism, a characteristic of Jews and Christians. Many years later, this polytheistic worship center would become the focal point of Muslim worship (monotheistic) after Mohammed's successful military conquest of Mecca.

In the year 610, at age forty, Mohammed retreated for relaxation to a cave on Mount Hira, not far from Mecca. He later stated that the angel Gabriel appeared to him and began sharing with him revelation from Allah, designed for the tribes around Mecca. The visions continued from 610 through A.D.

622. Reaction to Mohammed in Mecca was less than enthusi-
astic. Mohammed's claims that he was a prophet of Allah
sent to reclaim a wicked and fallen people produced few followers and brought much scorn and ridicule. However, his
loving wife, Khadija, believed in him. When Mohammed
shared with his wife that he was afraid that his visions might
even be demonic, she assured him they were from Allah. She
became the first convert to Islam. Zeyd, his adopted son, and
Ali, a cousin, also embraced Mohammed's views. Soon, forty
persons were following Islam, which means "submission."

But Mohammed was not well received among most of
Mecca's inhabitants. Mohammed was unpopular among
Mecca's pagans (who preferred worshiping the 360 "gods" in
the Ka'bah). He called himself a "prophet" in hopes that
Jews would accept him. They did not. He labeled himself an
"apostle" with the hope that Christians would embrace him.
But they didn't either.

So unenthused were residents of Mecca to embrace
Mohammed that a fight broke out in which Zeyd, Mohammed's
adopted son, was struck. In an ominous statement, Anis
Shorrosh has stated that this was the first time blood had
been spilled in behalf of Islam."[6] As rejections of Islam intensified, some of Mohammed's followers fled to Abyssinia—
present-day Ethiopia—for purposes of safety.

THE ORIGIN OF "ALLAH"

As opposition turned hostile toward Mohammed and his
teachings, he made one of his most controversial decisions.
As the citizens of Mecca were laying siege to his portion of
the city, he temporarily compromised his monotheistic
stance. Although the story is difficult to decipher, it appears
that he agreed to worship the three daughter-gods of the

sun (Al-Lat, Al-Uzza, and Manat) and the moon (Allah). He later retracted this position, saying Satan had influenced him. These statements, taken from Sura 53:19 in the Koran, led to the controversy of the "satanic verses" which catapulted author Salman Rushdie into the global limelight in February of 1989.

MANY MARRIAGES

When his beloved wife of 25 years, Khadija, died, Mohammed was fifty years of age and had been on his mission for ten years. He grieved deeply at her loss. However, within two months, he married Sawda, who was followed by fifteen women whom he would take as wives, all at the same time: Aisha, Omm Salma, Hafsa, Zaynab (of Jahsh), Jowayriya, Omm Habiba, Safiya, Maymuna (of Hareth), Fatema, Hend, Asma (of Saba), Zaynab (of Khozayma), Habla, Asma (or Noman), along with two more who were slaves or concubines, Mary (the Coptic) and Rayhana.[7]

The large cadre of wives and other women is the explanation for certain verses in the Koran, allegedly given to Mohammed by Allah, directing his wives to "get along with each other."

There are stories—both horrible and fascinating—surrounding some of the wives. Aisah was only seven—or perhaps nine—years of age when Mohammed married her. In another instance, Zaynab was the wife of Zeyd, Mohammed's adopted son. Mohammed walked in on her once while she was "unveiled." He was taken by her beauty. Zeyd consequently divorced her so that Mohammed could marry her. This is the reason for al-Ahzab 33:37 in the Koran, in which Allah supposedly commands Zeyd to divorce his wife so that Mohammed could marry her.

When Mohammed's many wives became jealous of Mary, the Coptic (Egyptian) Christian slave girl, Mohammed punished them by spending the next month with Mary alone. Another wife, Safiya, was just fifteen when Mohammed married her. She was taken from the Jewish settlement of Khaibar after Mohammed had attacked it.

Zaynab, not to be confused with the Zaynab who had previously been married to Mohammed's son-in-law, was Jewish. She had been taken as a wife as a result of a bloody battle. She planned to revenge the deaths of her husband, her father, and her brother by poisoning Mohammed.

Cooking the poison into some meat, she gave it to Mohammed and his friends. He promptly recognized the taste of poison and spit it out. One of his friends was not so fortunate and died. Zaynab defended herself, saying that if he were really a prophet, he would have refused the meat, knowing that it was poisoned. Although the poison never took Mohammed's life, it did affect his health and, in all probability, contributed to his death several years later in 632.

FROM MECCA TO MEDINA

Mohammed's life, however, was much more than marriages and wives. His "calling" from the angel Gabriel was to address the wickedness and polytheism of Mecca. The non-receptivity of Mecca's pagans caused Mohammed to move his operations 270 miles north of Mecca to Yathrib, known today as Medina. His attraction to this area was the fact that twelve pagans in that city had accepted Islam. In their zeal, they spread the Muslim message. As the Yathrib numbers grew, they asked Mohammed to send a teacher. Forced out of Mecca, Mohammed had gone to a cave outside the town. At age fifty-three, Mohammed was a man without a home, with only a few followers (in Yathrib), driven to hiding in a cave for three days.

On the fourth day, July 16, 622, Mohammed left for Yathrib. This date marks the beginning of the Muslim calendar—the date of the "flight" or the "Hegira." Thus this year is delineated as "1 A.H."("After the Hegira.").[8]

With the rejection of Islam in Mecca, Mohammed was quite glad to go to a city where a group of devotees not only announced their allegiance to him but also placed their lives and properties at his disposal. Yathrib, at Mohammed's direction, was renamed Medina and became the headquarters of his operations for the next eight years.

The Koran itself reflects the changing nature of Islam at this time. Mohammed's earliest Mecca-based writings were essentially peaceful in content, with few negative reactions to Christians and Jews. In fact, he had assumed that Christians and Jews would embrace his teachings since they were monotheistic. But, upon his move to Medina and because of the battles that followed, the writings take on a considerably more militant and violent tone.

MEDINA

After arriving in Medina, Mohammed built a great mosque. But his life was more consumed with wars and skirmishes. In the Battle of Badr, he overtook a Quraysh caravan. The Quraysh were his own tribal group from Mecca who had not accepted him. Some were executed. Those who announced their allegiance to Allah were spared. This marked what would become a hallmark of Muslim expansion—the coercive, "evangelistic" potential of the sword. Mohammed's use of the sword was justified by the fact that he was Allah's commissioned prophet to enforce "truth."

Mohammed returned to Medina a hero. The use of the sword to advance his cause had not been forgotten. The account is chilling.

A woman called Asma, whose family still followed their ancestral faith, composed verses which pointed out that to follow Mohammed was to follow a man who had killed many of his own people in battle. These verses made sure that her dislike of Islam was no secret.

Others must have felt the same way since the verses spread quickly through Medina by word of mouth. When the Muslims heard them, they took offense. A Muslim by the name Umair made a public vow to kill Asma. He stabbed her with his sword as she slept with her children one night, taking ironic care to remove her nursing baby before pinning her to the couch. Mohammed himself was aware of Umair's intentions. The next morning Umair approached him in the mosque at prayer to notify him that Asma had paid for her refusal to accept Islam.

Asma's clan confronted Umair, who threatened the clan with death if they did not convert. The whole clan converted to avoid being killed.[9]

And thus grew Islam, even in its earliest days.

MEDINA AND THE JEWS

Jews from Syria had settled Medina originally. Once again, Mohammed was determined to win the Jews' allegiance; and once again he failed. They would not acknowledge him as the teacher from Abraham. Where persuasion failed, the sword would succeed.

The Jews, primarily working as goldsmiths, lived in a small fort outside the city. Mohammed informed them that they must acknowledge him as a prophet of God or be prepared to pay a price. After an unsuccessful attempt to defend themselves, they were brought out one by one. Pleading for mercy, they were told they could live but must leave the city. Mohammed and his followers took the Jews' possessions and homes.

Back in Mecca, there was a call to avenge what Mohammed had done to the Quraish caravan members. Three thousand men marched from Mecca to settle the score with Mohammed. In the confusion of battle, the cry went up, mistakenly, that "Mohammed is slain!" Although injured, he had most certainly not been slain, as Mecca would painfully learn. This event only proved to reinforce Mohammed's invincibility.

A second attempt to seek revenge upon Mohammed and Medina with 10,000 warriors from Mecca also failed. In one year, the sixth year of the Hegira, Mohammed led seventeen different expeditions, capturing livestock and wealth. The name of Islam now spread fear.

THE QURAIZA JEWS

With 3,000 men, Mohammed pursued 2,000 outnumbered and "outgunned" Quraiza Jews. Overcome, the Jews surrendered. Mohammed declared that the men should be killed and the women and children sold into slavery. Horrified women and children watched as the men were beheaded, in groups of five or six at a time. The slaughter lasted almost twenty-four hours, and the Muslims lit torches to continue into the night.[10] The name of Islam now spread even greater fear.

MECCA—THE ULTIMATE VICTORY

January 1, 630, was a day of impending calamity for the town that had rejected the founder of Islam. With 10,000 men, Mohammed marched triumphantly into Mecca, the city too overwhelmed by the Islamic forces to even defend itself. He circled the Ka'bah seven times and ordered the destruction of the 360 idols in the temple. Earlier, in an apparent attempt to woo Jewish followers, Mohammed had insisted that prayers should be said facing Jerusalem. Now, as conqueror of Mecca, he declared that all prayers should be said facing toward the Ka'bah (or towards the city of Mecca), a practice followed by Muslims to this day. With Mecca conquered, warring Muslims fanned out to nearby communities, killing entire tribes who resisted worshiping Allah.

In 632, the tenth year of the Hegira, sixty-three-year old Mohammed took his entourage of wives and followers to Mecca. More than one hundred choice camels were sacrificed for this special occasion. After completing several religious rituals, he returned to Medina.

HIS SICKNESS AND DEATH

In mid-632, Mohammed became ill. Part of his loss of health was caused by the lingering impact of the poison that Zaynab had given him. For two weeks, his fever soared. Saturday seemed worse. Sunday, he lingered. Monday brought some hoped-for improvement, which allowed him to be taken one more time to the mosque. But later that day, alone with wife Aisha, Mohammed died. The date was June 8, 632. His body was washed. A grave was dug where he lay, and his body was lowered into it. Second only to the mosque in Mecca, this Medina burial site is the most holy place in the Islamic tradition.

GROWTH OF THE ISLAMIC EMPIRE

After the death of Mohammed in 632, four different Khalifs (sometimes "Caliphs," meaning "successors") provided leadership to the burgeoning religious group. Abu Bakr, father-in-law of Mohammed, ruled as successor for 2 years, from 632-4.

Umar (All of their names are shortened here.) was caliph for 10 years, from 634-44. During this time Islam overtook Iraq, Syria, Egypt, and the city of Jerusalem (A.D. 638) where the Dome of the Rock Mosque was later built (691) on the site where the Jewish temple had stood. (The taking of the Holy Land by the Muslims later sparked the "Christian" Crusades in 1098.) Umar was assassinated in 644.

Uthman ruled for 12 years, from 644-56, the year he was assassinated. Ali (a relative of Mohammed) became the caliph in 656, at which time a Muslim Civil War broke out. He was murdered in 661. As we shall see later, the selection of the caliph created a breach within Islam—Sunnis vs. Shi'ites—that has never healed.

TWO DYNASTIES: UMAYYADS AND ABBASIDS

In 661, Damascus became the capital of the Umayyad Dynasty, the "family" of leaders of the expanding Islamic Empire. They extended their influence into what is now Russia and reached the borders of China. The sweep across North Africa continued all the way to the shores of the Atlantic Ocean. Islam was now truly multinational.

In 750, another Arab family (The Abbasids) overthrew the Damascus-based Islamic leadership and moved the capital of the Islamic Empire to Baghdad (present-day Iraq) in 762. Islam controlled an enormous landmass extending from India on the east to Spain on the west. The Abbassids killed almost every member of the Umayyads except one who escaped to Spain.

ADVANCES IN SPAIN AND FRANCE

Meanwhile, Islamic armies were moving across Spain and in 713 reached Narbonne, France. Spain was largely Muslim. Cordova, Spain, with a population of 100,000, had 700 mosques. By 732, Muslims had moved within 170 miles of Paris, population 30,000 at the time.

In the famous Battle of Tours (or Poitiers) in 732, Charles Martel (grandfather of Charlemagne) defeated the Muslims, a turning point in both Christian and Islamic history. Had it not been for Martel's victory, many of you reading this book would be using the Koran rather than the Bible in your worship services.

Former Israeli Prime Minister Netanyahu has stated that part of the present-day Islamic conflicts is the result of having been driven back in 732. (Over the next 300 years, Muslims were driven back in Spain. The last Muslim stronghold in Spain, Granada, fell in 1492.) The end of the 700s marks the "golden age" for Islam, a time of outstanding educational accomplishments in science, astronomy, and mathematics.

LOCALIZED RULERS

After 935, the Abassids were officially regarded, but there were many local or regional caliphs (as caliphs did not hold temporal power from 935 onwards) who have names that seem strange to us:

* The Samanids, 874-999 (Persia, Iran)
* The Spanish Kindom of al-Andalus, 912-61

* The Hamdanids, 929-1003 (Arabia)

* The Buwayids, 930-1030 (Western Iran, Southern Iraq)

* The Ikshids, 935-69 (Western Iran, Egypt, Syria)

* The Shi'ite Fatimids, 969-1171 (Northern Africa)

* The Ghaznavids, 967-1030 (India)

* The Seljuk Turks, 990-1118 ("Seljuk" was the name of a tribal chief; "Turks" applies to an area in Central Asia, larger than present-day Turkey) (Western Iran, Syria, Byzantine)

THE CRUSADES

The Seljuk Turks were fierce fighters. That fact caused the leader of the Eastern part of the Christian Church in Constantinople (now called Istanbul), Turkey, to call for help from Pope Urban II in Rome. He responded in 1098 by calling for persons to form armies to reclaim the Holy Land. By 1099, a rather vagabond "Christian" army had taken Jerusalem and held it from 1099 to 1291, establishing the Latin Kingdom of Jerusalem.

GENGHIS KHAN AND THE MONGOLS

The Crusaders, however, were nothing compared to the force that swept down from China: the Mongols. By 1258, they overran Baghdad, thus ending the Islamic Abbasid Empire that had begun five hundred years earlier, in 750. The Mongols took Iraq and Syria and headed toward Egypt.

THE MAMLUK WARRIORS

Near Nazareth (Jesus' hometown in Israel), the well-trained Mamluks military force from Egypt met the seemingly intractable Mongols and successfully routed them in 1260, the first army ever to defeat the Mongols in open battle.

THE OTTOMAN TURKS

The Mamluks likewise seemed to be undefeatable, until they encountered the Ottoman Turks, who ruled for four hundred years, from the early 1500s until World War I in 1917. Under a chieftain name Othman, these Turkish-speaking warriors were also Islamic and had been driven from their homeland by the Mongols mentioned above. (Although not identical, the terms "Ottoman Empire" and "Turkey" are often used interchangeably.) The Ottomans defeated the Mamluks in 1517 and then conquered Egypt, Syria, Rhodes, Vienna, Hungary, Cyprus, Crete, and Iraq. But the Ottomans also faced many setbacks: loss of Kiev, Vienna, Russia, and Egypt; Serbian revolt (1815); financial bankruptcy (1861-76); a palace coup (1876); Arab revolt (1916-21); and the Turkish War of independence (1919-21).

WORLD WAR I

During WWI, the Ottomans sided with the Germans and were defeated by the Allied Forces, specifically the British. At this point, Muslims had controlled Palestine (Israel) almost continually from A.D. 636 until 1917 (for 1300 years) when the British took control.

THE ISRAELI—PALESTINIAN CONFLICT

At the end of World War I, 92 percent of the population of Palestine was Arab, who claim to descend from Ishmael. Jews (descendents of Isaac), who were looking for a place to call home, longed to be in Israel, which had been their land from 1400 B.C. (when Joshua led them into Canaan) to A.D. 70 (the New Testament period). In 1897, the first Zionist conference was held in Basel, Switzerland, in order to attempt to create a Jewish state in the Ottoman province of Palestine. Now the opportunity afforded itself in World War I. The Jewish people seized the moment (due to the friendly British troops) and established a "beachhead" in Israel once again. Three decades later, in 1948, Israel once again became a recognized nation with a land of its own—the land promised them by God so many centuries ago.

More than 750,000 Palestinians fled the country when Israel became a Jewish state. "Palestine" was a term given to Israel by the Romans when they destroyed Jerusalem in A.D. 70, during New Testament times, for the purpose of destroying the Jews and making certain that there would never be another nation called Israel. But the Jews *did* come back. And they *did* call it Israel. And the Palestinian Arabs (who had lived there from the destruction of Jerusalem in A.D. 70 till the end of World War I in 1917) were equally determined to claim it for their homeland.

The humiliating defeat of Arab nations by Israel in the 1967 Six Day War galvanized the pro-Palestinian (and Muslim) movement and served to reenergize the radical Islamic cause. Anti-Israeli feelings rose to a fever pitch. Attempts at "democratization" of Muslim countries faded, being replaced by the "Islamic Resurgence" of radical fundamentalism from 1970 to the present. "Secularist" (pro-democratic or Western forms of government) policies were replaced by a strict, rigid application of Islamic law, often accompanied by militancy and violence.

This brief look at the descendants (or at least the alleged descendants, in the case of Ishmael) of the two sons of

Abraham—Isaac and Ishmael—shines light on today's conflicts. As we will see in the next chapter, Muslims feel it is their religious duty to convert the rest of the world to Islam, whether it is through peaceful or violent means. And the tiny nation of Israel, the one ethnic group singled out (in biblical times) by God as "His" people, stands in the way of this conquest.

THE SOLUTION?

The conflict will continue unless we as Christians, lovingly articulate the good news of Christ in such an effective way that both Jews and Arabs accept Him as Lord—thus causing them to "realign" their thinking as brothers and sisters in Christ.

I dream too big, you say? Unrealistic, you think? (See last chapter for ways to share Christ with Muslims). Well, I'm not the one who came up with the idea. In Matthew 28, Jesus instructed us to "go" for the purpose of discipling every ethnic group (original language: *ethnos)*. And that includes Israelis (Jews) and Palestinians (Muslims).

CHAPTER FOUR

ISLAM AND THE KORAN

Who are the Muslims? What is Islam? What do Muslims believe? How do they worship? What does their "holy book," the Koran (sometimes spelled "Quran"), really say?

BELIEFS

Muslims have five main beliefs:

* Belief in Allah as the one true God.

* Belief in angels as instruments of God's will, specifically bringing the words of the Koran to Mohammed.

* Belief in the Koran as an infallible book.

* There are many prophets (including Moses and Jesus), but Mohammed is the last prophet.

* Everyone will be judged by Allah. Paradise and Hell await the blessed and the damned.

PRACTICES

A Muslim must practice the "five pillars":

* The Creed (Shahada): "There is no God but Allah, and Mohammed is the messenger of God."

* Daily Prayers (Salat), praying five times a day: (1) rising of the sun, (2) noon, (3) midafternoon, (4) sunset, and (5) before going to bed. Whereas many Christians worship on Sundays and Jews celebrate the Sabbath on

Saturdays, Muslims have public prayer services on Fridays. These services are primarily for men only.

* The Fast of Ramadan: Fasting occurs during the daylight hours of Ramadan. The Muslim calendar is based on the lunar year; thus Ramadan can fall in winter or summer.

* Almsgiving (Zakat): Muslims are to give 2.5% (one fortieth) of one's wealth. Almsgiving was voluntary in early Islam. It is mandatory in contemporary Islam.

* The Pilgrimage (Hajj) to Mecca: Muslims are required (unless health prohibits it) to make one visit to Mecca in their lifetime, a city that only Muslims are allowed to enter.

ISLAM TO BE SPREAD BY JIHAD

There is an "unofficial" sixth pillar of Islam, particularly of fundamentalist Muslims: jihad. The term "jihad" means "struggle" and can mean something as innocuous as the personal internal struggle to obey God or the struggle against the devil. Unfortunately, it can be something as violent as killing those who do not accept Islam. Jihad has four potential expressions:[11]

* Jihad of the tongue: talking about Islam

* Jihad of the hand: good works

* Jihad of the heart: living the Islamic faith

These first three do not sound all that different from the language of Christianity. However, it is the fourth use of the term "jihad" that highlights the violent component of Islam.

* Jihad of the sword: defending Islam and, as many persons have come to experience in Muslim countries, attacking in the name of Allah—including such things as kidnappings and bombings.

THE TERMS "ISLAM" AND "MUSLIM"

Islam is the belief system. A Muslim is a person who follows the religion of Islam. Islam means "submission," specifically "submission to Allah." Tragically, as shall be seen later, it has come to mean "subjection" or even "subjugation."

BRANCHES OF ISLAM

Just as Christianity has its "denominations," Islam has approximately 150 different branches. They tend to fall into three main groups:

* Sunni, comprising 83 percent of Muslims; they follow the sayings and actions of Mohammed which were collected after his death in the books of the Hadith, which helps to interpret how to practically live out the Koran; in contrast to the Shi'ites, they believe that leaders (such as the ones that followed Mohammed) should be selected by a consensus of the community.

* Shia, or Shi'ites, approximately 16 percent of Muslims, located primarily in Iran and Iraq, follow a charismatic imam (spiritual leader); they have their own collections of the Hadith; they objected to the first three successors of Mohammed, feeling that succession should have remained in the family—specifically Ali, the son-in-law of Mohammed; thus they did not accept the first three caliphs (Abu Bakr, Umar, and Uthman).

* Sufis, a mystical group, search for union with God; it might be compared to the "charismatic" wing of Christianity—both in fervor and in distribution; this group is not necessarily a separate group but rather is found as a part of other branches of Islam (Sunni and Shia) much like the charismatic movement has spread across all Christian denominations.[12]

THE KORAN

The "holy scripture" of Islam is the Koran. Muslims believe it was given to Mohammed by the angel Gabriel as a direct translation of a book that is kept in Heaven. The book was given to Mohammed over a period of years in the Arabic language. Muslims see the Koran as the express image of God, similar to how Christians see Jesus as the Word of God. To them, Koran is such a divine book that many Muslim scholars refuse to allow it to be translated from the original Arabic.

The Koran is organized into 114 surahs (sometimes spelled surats) or chapters. It is quite confusing to most Christians, because we are used to reading the Bible, which is generally chronological in structure—from the "beginning" in Genesis to the "ending" in Revelation.

First-time readers can become easily confused because the 114 chapters are written in non-chronological order. They are organized strictly by length—from longest to shortest. Thus, the earliest written Mecca-based passages, approximately A.D. 612-22 (friendly to Christians and Jews), are interspersed with the later Medina-based writings, approximately A.D. 622-32 (at times, violent towards Christians, Jews, and others).

Since there is a tendency for persons to "speak longer" the older they get, it has been assumed by some that the shorter chapters were actually early writing, and the longer ones are later writings. If that is true, then the book is actually arranged backwards: latest (longest) writings towards the front; early (shortest) writings towards the back. However, even this theory does not always hold, for in some surahs there is a mixture of Meccan (early) and Medinan (late) writings.

The earliest written copies of the Koran (often transcribed by Mohammed's followers) were on leaves, stones, pieces of bark, and even bones. Some of these materials were biodegradable and over time were partially or totally degraded, with the writing becoming obscured. Other materials (such as leaves) were actually eaten away by animals. Thus the task of accumulating the entire Koran was no small task. A complete manuscript of the Koran was compiled by Hafasa (one of Mohammed's widows), approximately twenty years after his death. The Koran was first printed in Arabic at Rome in 1530, followed by a French translation in 1647 and an English translation in 1657.[13]

Another unique feature of the Koran is its frequent repetition. The book was originally written with the purpose of being memorized (by uneducated persons). While the repetition is helpful for memory purposes, it can seem tedious to read.

One more confusing point: Muslims state that the Koran is always in the "first person," that is, Allah is always the one speaking. However, there are clearly some portions where that is not the case. In those portions, Mohammed is speaking. This only adds to the confusion of first-time readers.

THE BIBLE VS. THE KORAN

Many Christian readers of the Koran are surprised by the number of times in which the Koran cites biblical names or accounts. However, one of the most difficult components of the Koran is the historical inaccuracy when quoting accounts from the Bible. The Koran speaks highly of the Bible in some texts and refers to Jews and Christians as "the people of the Book." But, at the same time, there are numerous historical errors. Bear in mind that the Bible was written many years before the Koran. The surviving Old Testament manuscripts date back to 200 B.C. Existing New Testament manuscripts date back to the first century A.D. The Koran was not written until the 600s. Thus the Koran borrowed many biblical stories, yet scrambled dates and details.

INACCURACIES OF BIBLICAL HISTORY IN THE KORAN

Here are just a few examples of the many inaccuracies found within the Koran:

1. The Bible states that all of Noah's sons went into the Ark. The Koran states (Surah 11:32-48) that one drowned.

2. There are many mistakes regarding Abraham, but only a few will be mentioned here. Abraham had 8 sons according to the Bible, not 2 as the Koran states. The Koran claims that Abraham went to Mecca. There is no biblical or archaeological support for this story. The Koran also states that Nimrod threw Abraham into the fire (Surahs 21:68-9 and 9:69). However, Nimrod lived several hundred years before Abraham.

3. The following are portrayed as living during the same time: Haman and Moses, Mary and Aaron. The flood is portrayed as occurring during the same time as Moses. The Tower of Babel and Pharaoh are lumped into the same time frame.

4. Of the four glaring errors regarding Moses, I'll mention but one: Moses was adopted by Pharaoh's daughter, not his wife (Surah 28:8-9; Exodus 2:5).

5. There are at least five errors listed regarding Mary, two of which are as follows: Mohammed confused Mary with Miriam, the sister of Moses. The Koran also states that Mary gave birth under a palm tree, not in a stable (Surah 19:22; Luke 2:1-20).

6. The account regarding soldiers getting a drink of water occurred under Gideon, not when David was fighting Goliath (Surah 2:249-250; Judges 7:1-8).

The obvious question is how did these (and so many other errors) make it into the Koran? It must be remembered that Mohammed did not have a Bible. An Arabic translation of the Bible did not exist during his lifetime. He would have listened to the stories told around late-night campfires during times of herding sheep (when he was young) and as the caravans of traders—Jewish, Christian, and pagan—came through Mecca. The stories (without written form to sustain them) were apparently "jumbled," both chronologically and in details.

How do Muslims view these apparent contradictions to the Bible? According to Islam, the Bible (although written hundreds of years before the Koran) was "corrupted" and thus is not reliable. Where the Bible agrees with the Koran, so goes the logic, the Bible is correct. If the Bible and the Koran disagree, then the Bible has been corrupted and is wrong. How do they know that? Because Allah says so. And how do they know that Allah says so? Because the Koran says that what Allah says is true. Thus goes the circular logic.

SOURCES OF THE KORAN

The difficulty in reading the Koran is not merely its non-chronological structure or the difficult means by which it was recorded and compiled. Sources that Mohammed frequently "borrowed" from were Arabian fables, Jewish stories (from the Talmud, Midrash, and apocryphal writings), and occasional Zoroastrian and Hinduistic stories. Mohammed even incorporated stories into the Koran that came from books that were rejected by the early Church fathers from inclusion in the New Testament. Some of the "Gnostic Gospels," as they are called, appeared during the third century and were widely distributed from the fourth through the seventh centuries. One of these was the apocryphal account of Jesus as a youth entertaining others by turning a piece of clay into a real bird (Surah 3:49). There is even a story of Jesus speaking while he was a baby in the cradle (Surah 3:46). The New Testament, written six hundred years before the Koran, has no such stories.

THE HADITH

Most people understand the Koran is to a Muslim what the Bible is to a Christian. That is a simple analogy and easy for us to understand. What is not known by many Westerners is that the Hadith (the Tradition), a multi-volume work, is regarded as being nearly as holy and authoritative as the Koran. The Hadith is a collection of sayings that are attributed to Mohammed regarding how to live the Muslim life. After these sayings were gathered, early Muslim leaders tried to determine which ones were authentic. Many of the sayings were rejected and thus are not part of the Hadith. That accounts for the fact that the Sunni Muslims and the Shia Muslims do not have the same exact collections of the Hadith.

"ISLAM" AND ALLAH, ISLAM'S GOD

Mohammed did not invent the term "Islam." It existed in Arabia before Mohammed created his religion. It referred to the strength, courage, and tenacity of a desert warrior willing to fight to the death for the sake of his tribe. Over time, the term "Islam" came to mean "submission." It does not, as some contemporary Muslims like to claim, mean "peace."

Like the term "Islam," "Allah" (as a term) existed in the pre-Islamic times. "Allah" comes from two Arabic words put together: *al* (the) and *ilih* (god). Mohammed's father's name even included the term. His name was Abdullah, or Abd-Allah, meaning "God's servant." His uncle's name was Obied-Allah.

Where does the term "Allah" come from? One theory is as follows: In pre-Islamic Arabia, the sun was regarded as a goddess. The moon, while worshiped in the Ancient Near East as a female goddess, was worshiped in Arabia as a male god called Allah. When the moon god Allah married the sun goddess, they produced the three "daughters of Allah": Al-Lat, Al-Ussa, and Manat. (The crescent moon came to be used as an Islamic symbol during the Ottoman period—1500-1900—but the actual origin is not known for certain.) The moon god and the three daughters were worshiped in the Quraysh tribe in which Mohammed was raised. In fact, two of the three "daughters" had the female version of the name "Allah," the moon god. This fact, according to this theory, made it easier for the Arabs of Mohammed's day to embrace the concept of "Allah."

It is not clear whether "Allah," as a word, was indigenous to Arabian culture or was borrowed from the Hebrew or Syriac languages. Although the origin is somewhat uncertain, "Allah" was a term that was likely used for "god" in pre-Islamic Arabia. Some scholars even believe that the term may have been used by Christians in Arabia before the time of Mohammed.[14]

THE GOD OF THE BIBLE AND ALLAH IN THE KORAN

"Allah" is the word for "god" in Arabic. But does that mean that when Muslims and Christians pray, we are praying to the same God?

No.

Why? The *character* or *description* of Allah in the Koran and the *character* or *description* of Jehovah in the Bible are not the same. Let me state it another way: the "content" of the word "Allah" to Muslims who believe the Koran and the "content" of the word "God" (or "Jehovah") to Christians who believe the Bible are not the same at all. The koranic revelation of Allah and the biblical revelation of Yahweh are in profound conflict. (In fact, they are so different that some believe that Arabic-speaking Christians should not use the term "Allah" to describe God and the Arabic Bible should not use "Allah" to depict God.)[15]

The same god could not give two opposing revelations of himself. When you consider that the revelations (holy scriptures) contradict each other, one is left with only two possible conclusions: (1) Either one is true and the other is false, or (2) Both are false. But it is irrational to suggest that one who is truly God would give two separate revelations that contradict each other. Thus (assuming that both the Koran and the Bible are not "false,") one is true and the other is false. Or, if they are both true, they are certainly not speaking of the same "god."

Christians who blindly say, "After all, we both serve the same God, we just call Him by different names," must decide: Which God do you believe? Simply stated, the Christian Jehovah and the Muslim Allah are not the same. Here is why.

Because Christianity and Islam are both monotheistic ("one god"), many incorrectly assume that the two faiths must be quite similar. There are *some* similarities, including a respected role of Abraham, Moses, and Jesus; respect for the prophetic gifting; and a call for moral living. However, the dissimilarities are significant. The God of the Bible is very personal and intimately involved in the history of mankind. This is called "theism" (God intertwined with history). The Islamic view of God is "deistic" (God created but disengaged from the earth's daily affairs). Allah is impersonal and not involved *providentially*. In fact, one of the major characteristics of Islam is its fatalism. To Christians, "the Lord willing" speaks of His "hand" on history. To Muslims, "God willing" is surrender to a type of "what will be, will be."

Another important difference between Christianity and Islam is our entrance into Heaven. For Christians, salvation comes through the unmerited forgiveness offered us by God, based on the sacrificial death of Jesus, the Son of God. We believe what Jesus taught His disciples, as recorded in the Gospel of John: *"I am the way, the truth, and the life. No one can come to the Father except through me"* (John 14:6 NLT). The God of the Bible is a God of grace. One cannot earn salvation. It is a free gift. In the teachings of Islam, however, one must earn salvation by works. One's deeds done on earth will be weighed in judgment to determine the type of afterlife that has been earned.

Here is a crucial point in understanding why the God of the Bible and Allah in Islam are not one and the same. Christians hold to a theology that proclaims God to be three-in-one: the Trinity. Can Christians explain this one God who proclaims Himself to be three distinct persons? No—it is a mystery. But that does not make it false. The concept of the trinity is an offense to Muslims. In the Bible, God is known in three distinct persons (while at the same time being one): Father, Son, and Holy Spirit. Muslims cannot comprehend this. They view Christians as "tri-theists" (worship of three distinct gods). In fact, some Muslims misunderstand the trinity to be God (the Father),

Jesus, and Mary (as opposed to the Holy Spirit). God is either a triune being or He is not. Christians believe He is; Muslims believe in a god who is not triune. This issue relates back to the God of Christians being a personal God. He is Father, Son, and Holy Spirit—a community. There is relationship between the Three; thus, there can be relationship between God and us.

In order to believe that Jehovah and Allah are one and the same, you would have to believe that:

* God is both deeply personal *and* highly impersonal;

* Salvation is based entirely on unmerited grace offered through the sacrificial death of God Himself *and* is based entirely on the works one does on earth;

* God is three complete, individual personalities in one—Father, Son, and Holy Spirit—while at the same time is repulsed by the idea of being anything but one complete person.

The God of the Bible and Allah of the Koran are not the same. A former Muslim has stated emphatically that an intellectually honest follower of Islam would never say Jehovah God and Allah are the same since the Koran specifically teaches that Allah has no son. And faithful Muslims would never say that they are the same either since to them, God had no son. To them, Jesus and the Holy Spirit are not a part of the Godhead. Need more evidence? Let's look at how the Bible and the Koran differ in their description of Jesus.

ISLAM, THE KORAN, AND JESUS

Jesus is just one among twenty-five prophets mentioned in the Koran. Mohammed is the last of the prophets. Many Christians are surprised to learn that the Koran teaches that Jesus had a miraculous conception, something

Christians affirm as the virgin birth. The Koran contains a bizarre account of Jesus speaking at His birth. However, the Bible contradicts such an account, noting that Jesus' first miracle was at a wedding in Canaan. The Koran correctly states that Jesus was sinless, had supernatural knowledge, was empowered by the Holy Spirit, and was the Word of God. Furthermore, Jesus served, healed, and even raised people from the dead. And, amazingly, the Jesus of the Koran ascended into Heaven and will return to earth. In fact, Jesus ('Isa) is mentioned 97 times in 93 verses of the Koran. Of all the prophets, Jesus makes it into the list of the six most significant prophets:

* Adam, the Chosen of God

* Noah, the Preacher of God

* Abraham, the Friend of God

* Moses, the Speaker of God

* Jesus, the Word of God

* Mohammed, the Apostle of God[16]

Then where, a Christian might ask, do the Bible and the Koran disagree regarding Jesus? The answer to that question is the most important part of Christian belief: *the death, burial, and resurrection of Jesus.* The Bible teaches that Jesus died a sacrificial death, defeating sin, the grave, and death. Muslims find it offensive that God would come in the form of a man (They would say, "God has no son.") and even more ridiculous that He would die on a cross. Thus, the Koran teaches that somehow, someone took Jesus' place, so He did not actually die on the cross. While there is not universal agreement among Muslim theologians, one of the theories is that Judas somehow took on the form of Jesus, thus Judas was crucified. Everyone simply *thought* it was Jesus.

Another one of the views is that one of Jesus' friends, whom God caused to resemble Jesus, was crucified in Jesus' place.

Remember, there is no sacrificial cross in Islam. And without the sacrifice on the cross, there is no atonement for our sins, no forgiveness, no free gift of salvation. And without the free gift of salvation, there are, in its place, works. Muslims must practice the "Five Pillars" of the faith in hope of reaching Paradise. Muslims don't believe in the Christian understanding of "original sin" (the distinct human bent towards sinning and wrongdoing). They believe in such a thing as sinful "acts" but not a sinful "nature." On the issue of salvation, Christianity and Islam do not merely hold *dissimilar* views. They hold *opposite* views.

ISLAM'S MANY "PARTS"

Mohammed was not just a religious guide. He and the writings he left behind also functioned as a military guide, as well as a force for social and political change.[17] Thus, Islam needs to be viewed through each of those "lenses." America Christians, who are uninitiated in Islamic ways, incorrectly assume that Islam is "merely a religion." They often fail to see the multifaceted nature of this religious-legal-military-political force.

ISLAM AS A RELIGION

In the religion of Islam are many strong moral teachings. In spite of the historical record of coercion and killing, there are many noble teachings in Islam. One has to respect those who pray multiple times daily. How few Christians do that! In fact, there are several points of "intersection" between Christianity and Islam. Muslims share with Christians the

belief that individual lives will be judged with the results of
the judgment being Heaven (Paradise) or Hell (although the
Islamic Paradise and the Christian Heaven differ greatly).
Muslims share with Christians a respect for the writings of
Moses, the Psalms (writings of David), and the Gospels.
(Muslims, however, feel that the present-day biblical accounts
are "corrupted.") One has to admire Mohammed's commit-
ment to monotheism in the midst of a polytheistic culture.

A Muslim's stance on alcohol, immorality, pornography,
and abortion is admirable and correct. In fact, it would be
spectacular if Christians were as outspoken on such issues
as Muslims are. Islamic respect for sexual purity is
admirable and, once again, right. (The consequences for violations in the sexual realm are extremely severe, for both
fornication and adultery.) The Hadith has many noble guidelines regarding family life. The Islamic welfare and philan-
thropic organizations, which provide for the poor and
downtrodden, deserve the respect of all. The Koran's respect
for other religions (specifically Jews and Christians), at least
in *early* koranic passages, is honorable.

For those who know only about the militarism of funda-
mentalist Islam, it is important to "counter" that perception
with some of the noble features of Islamic thought. Dr. J.
Dudley Woodberry has noted that some of the prayers of the
Sufi branch of Islam sound as if they were written by
Christian believers. Woodberry also observed that some of
the most pious persons he has ever known have been
Muslims, who were truly in search of God.[18]

But, Islam is *not* merely a religion in the way Americans
think of religion. It certainly is a religious "system" of beliefs,
as we have noted above, but it is so much more. It is a legal

system, a political force, a military regime, and a complete "culture" in itself.

INFLUENCER OF CULTURE

Islam is a cultural phenomenon. It is, simply put, a "'deification' (to make like a deity) of 7th century Arabian culture. In a very profound sense, Islam is more cultural than it is religious."[19] Islam often requires persons to adapt customs, styles, and fashions of the Arab world 1400 years ago. Middle Eastern Muslims, as a general rule, disdain the West and its cultural imperialism (American customs being forced on others). They portray their centuries-old customs and lifestyles as the way all should live—now and into the future. While it is true that Western cultural imperialism is wrong, 7th century Arabian 'cultural imperialism is also wrong.

ISLAMIC LAW

Islam is also a system of law known as the "sharia." There is no such thing as separation of church and state in Islam. That is why some countries are called *"Islamic* nations" or *"Muslim* nations." Nowhere in the world are there, at least by law, *Christian* nations. The Koran and other Muslim documents are the foundations for Islamic nations. Islam does not easily coexist alongside other religions long term, because it is a system of law, and, to many Muslims, those laws are to be applied to the entire country.

Coexistence occurs only when Islam is in the minority (as it currently is in America), when it lacks critical mass. At its core is the need to dominate all of life: personal life, family life, culture, society, religion, and government.[20]

Americans naïvely assume that Islam is simply like other religions, "to each his own." Islam is, at its core, not capable of allowing persons of other religions to simply worship as they choose.

Attempts by more secular or liberal Muslims to "democratize" (from the word "democracy," meaning to introduce basic freedoms in) their countries have not fared well in the last twenty years. Strict fundamentalist interpretations of the Koran and Hadith have prevailed governmentally in much of the contemporary Muslim world, resulting in harassment, persecution, and sometimes death for non-Muslims. Where liberal or moderate Muslims are in the majority, there is tolerance. Where conservative or fundamentalist Muslims predominate, tolerance of other religions is rare, spotty, and unpredictable.

Americans would do well to recognize that some Muslim immigrants have come to the U.S. to convert America and believe that America needs to be rescued by Islamic solutions to its moral failure.[21]

POLITICAL INFLUENCER

Islam is a political force and a social "change agent." Anayat Durrani, in an article regarding the rapid rise in the number of mosques in American, stated that "Mosques are not only centers for spirituality, they are now bases for political and social change."[22] One scholar has said that in terms of global domination, Islam is far more successful than movements for democracy because a party for political democracy cannot utilize Muslim institutions, such as the network of mosques throughout a nation, that act as a grassroots force for change. Democracy movements have no

such cover and, thus, are more easily controlled or elimi-
nated by the government.[23]

MILITARY FORCE

Islam is a military regime. If you have laws (the *shari'a*),
you must have some way to enforce those laws. That
requires military might. And if your "theology" is to dominate
the entire earth, that requires a military as well.

Military campaigns have been a part of Islam from its
earliest days, with Mohammed himself involved in as many
as sixty-six battles. To a Muslim, the whole world is divided
into two parts: (1) those who have experienced the "peace"
(domination) of Islam, and (2) those who are yet to be conquered. Until a nation is converted to become a Muslim
nation, it is considered a *Dar-ul-Harb,* or battlefield. Once it
has been converted, or its nonbelieving population killed or
vanquished, it becomes *Dar-us-Salaam,* a Land of Peace. To
a Muslim, the United States is currently a battlefield. And
those willing to fight and die in this battle are plentiful.

Many fundamentalist Middle Eastern mosques and radical
Islamic schools, as Westerners have seen in news broadcasts,
are "military training centers" for young boys to be taught
the value of jihad, with the accompanying goal of becoming
a martyr for Allah. With that martyrdom comes the promise
of Paradise, complete with wine and seventy-two virgins.

The majority of the world's wars today are Islamic-
driven conflicts. At the time of the writing of this book, 28
of the 30 plus wars today are Muslim related. You would
be hard pressed to identify a "hot spot" on the globe that
does not involve Muslims fighting either other Muslim
sects or tribes or fighting to vanquish non-Muslims. One
example would be the Sudan: more than two million

Christians have been killed by Muslims in Sudan within the past twenty years. Here are some other current battle-fields involving Muslims:

* Algeria, where Muslim fundamentalists are fighting the ruling military regime;

* Nigeria, where Muslims seek out and kill Christians;

* Chechnya, Daghestan, Albania, Bosnia, Tajikistan, and Uzbekistan have had to quell uprisings among radical Muslims bent on overthrowing the current governments;

* Indonesian Muslims are slaughtering Christians in East Timor;

* The Muslim population in India has reached 200 million, and civil war among Muslims and the majority Hindus is a greater possibility now than ever before.

* While working on this chapter, reports surfaced of 63,000 Indonesian Christians about to be annihilated by Laksar Jihad, an Islamic militia group. Following the capture of a Christian village, various news sources reported houses and churches being looted then burned, Christian women being raped, and any who could not leave the village were butchered or forcibly 'converted' to Islam.[24]

* In 2001 alone, there were 300 suicide bombers that attacked in 14 countries. This form of Islamic violence is the one which most concerns governmental leaders of many nations.[25]

Writing from Israel, Ari and Shira Sorko-Ram noted that although America and her allies say, "We are not at war with Islam, . . . (but) a powerful force known as radical Islam has declared war on us, whether we acknowledge it or not. . . . Radical Islam is absolutely, utterly and totally at war with the world's Western Democratic nations. . . . As impossible as it is to comprehend, radical Islam's goal is to destroy the democratic Free World physically and/or financially and to replace her with a fundamentalist Islamic world order."[26]

By far, the most disturbing article on this topic was written by Isreali political activist Moshe Feiglin, founder of The Jewish Leadership Movement. Feiglin led the campaign of mass civil disobedience against the Oslo accords in 1995 and is attempting to create a Judaism-based leadership for the state of Israel. He wrote a jolting article on September 28, 2001, entitled "Why America Has Already Lost the War:"

"I ask every American," the President continues, "during lunch time tomorrow to pray for all the injured, their families, and the American nation. Go to church, to the synagogue, to the mosque, and pray," ended the President.

"Did I hear right?" I ask the storekeeper. "Did he say mosque?" She nodded.

"At this very moment you've lost the war," I say to the astonished storekeeper, and started looking for what I need on the shelves.

America has lost the war. The Americans have made the same mistake as the Israelis, and just as Israel is retreating from one defeat to the next, so the Americans are now lined up on the track to disintegration.

When the black boxes of the hijacked airplanes are recovered, we will hear the pilots screaming "Allah Achbar" in the last moments before the crash. They slaughtered you in the name of Allah, and now the President calls on you to pray to him. . . .

America will never admit that it is involved in a war of cultures, in fact in a religious war. . . .

America will never admit it, and consequently will be unable to fight back. Just like the Israelis.

They fail to identify the enemy. They seek the terrorists just as Sharon is pursuing individual terrorists. They are pursuing the wasps instead of destroying the nest, because they are afraid of the nest. They are afraid of a real confrontation between their values and those of Islam. [27]

First, I pray he is wrong. Secondly, I pray that focus of the final chapter of this book will grip us all in such a way that we will find out how to reach out to Muslims with the Gospel.

VIOLENCE IN THE KORAN

No one single issue regarding Islam provokes argument more than the notion that Islam is either a peaceful religion or a violent religion. Some dogmatically state that Islam is a religion of peace and then back that up by referring to Muslims they have known, either here in America or in their travels to other counties. Others strongly assert that Islam is a religion of violence, and they support the thesis by pointing to violent texts in the Koran, a recitation of a violent acts committed by Muslim armies through the centuries, and by persecution of Christians occurring in Muslim nations today. Those who feel that Islam is a religion of peace feel that any reference to violence-prone texts in the Koran are surely verses being taken out of context. So, who is right? Is Islam a religion of peace? Or is it a religion that, when followed, produces violence?

Let me restate what I noted earlier: The best strategy for Christians to relate to Muslims is with love, tenderness, acts of kindness, and compassion, along with Holy Spirit-directed and prayerfully timed conversations about Jesus. But I do not believe we should approach the Christian-Muslim dialogue with syrupy sentimentality. We should be informed regarding Muslim beliefs (and there are admittedly so many different Islamic sects that this can be difficult), the Koran, Islamic history, and present-day Muslim nations' governmental regulations, specifically regarding Christians and Christianity. Perhaps, on this issue, it would be best to let the Koran speak for itself.

Below are some of the violent texts found in the Koran. Some contend that the following verses do not apply to Christians. They apply to idolaters (polytheists), who are to be given two choices: 1) surrender and become Muslim or 2) die. In contrast, Christians and Jews (The People of the Book) are given 3 choices: 1) surrender and become Muslim, 2) surrender and pay the non-Muslim tax, or 3) die. Thus the calls for "death to infidels," they say, do not apply to Christians.

To those who say, "Islam is a religion of peace," these texts are seen as having had a unique application to certain points of early Islamic history but are not applicable today. They would say that quoting these texts (as a way of proving that the Koran supports violence) is an abuse of the text, taking it out of context. They contend that the texts apply to periods of time when Mohammed was involved in battles with Jews and Christians during his later Medina years. However, to the growing fundamentalist, militant Islamic movements, these texts are not irrelevant. They are sources of inspiration for the ongoing battles that are occurring in so many countries. Scholars may debate the actual intention and contexts of these texts. I will simply list them. Here are some of the texts regarding violence, from both the Koran and the Hadith:

* When the sacred months are over, slay the idolaters wherever you find them. Arrest them, besiege them, and lie in ambush everywhere for them.

If they repent and take to prayer and render the alms levy, allow them to go their way. God is forgiving and merciful. *(Surah 9:5)*

* Strike terror into the enemies of God and your enemies. *(Surah 8:60)*

* Fight them and God will punish them by your hands, cover them with shame. *(at-Taubah 9:14)*

* I will instill terror into the hearts of the Unbelievers: smite ye above their necks and smite all their finger-tips off them . . . It is not ye who slew them; it was God. *(Surah 8:12,17)*

* Believers, take neither Jews nor Christians for your friends. They are friends with one another. Whoever of you seeks their friendship will become one of their number. Allah does not guide the wrongdoers. *(Surah 5:51)*

* Prophet, make war on the unbelievers and the hypocrites and deal rigorously with them. Hell shall be their home: an evil fate. *(Surah 9:73)*

* Fight against such of those to whom the Scriptures were given as believe neither in Allah nor the Last Day, who do not forbid what Allah and His apostle have forbidden and do not embrace the true faith until they pay tribute out of hand and are utterly subdued. *(Surah 9:29)*

* Mohammed is Allah's apostle. Those who follow him are ruthless to the unbelievers but merciful to one another. *(Surah 48:29)*

* Let those who would exchange the life of this world for the hereafter, fight for the cause of Allah; whether they die or conquer, We shall richly reward them. *(Surah 4:74)*

* Fight for the sake of Allah those that fight against you, but do not attack them first. Allah does not love the aggressors. Kill them wherever you find them. Drive them out of the places from which they drove you. Idolatry is worse than carnage. But do not fight them within the precincts of the Holy Mosque unless they attack you there. *(Surah 2:190-191)*

* Believers, why is it that when it is said to you "March in the cause of Allah" you linger slothfully in the land? Are you content with that life in preference to the life to come? Few indeed are the blessings of this life, compared to those of the life to come. *(Surah 9:38)*

* Whether unarmed or well equipped, march on and fight for the cause of Allah with your wealth and your persons. *(Surah 9:41)*

* If any one desires a religion other than Islam, never will it be accepted of him. *(Surah 3:85)*

* And fight them on, until there is no more tumult [seduction] or oppression, and there prevail justice and faith in God. *(Surah 2:193)*

* And if you are slain, or die in the way of Allah, forgiveness and mercy from Allah are far better than all they could amass. *(Surah 3:157)*

* Fight those who do not believe in Allah, nor in the latter day, nor do they prohibit what Allah and His Apostle have prohibited, nor follow the religion of truth, out of those who have been given the Book until they pay the tax in acknowledment of superiority and thy are in a state of subjection]. *(Surah 9:29)*

VIOLENCE FOUND IN THE HADITH

The second most revered Islamic writing is the Hadith. With the passage of years, many teachings and sayings developed. Eventually these sayings were written down in the Hadith ("tradition"). There is not general agreement among Muslims what should be included or excluded from the Hadith. Sunni's, for example, have a slightly different Hadith than the Shi'ites. The Hadith is also called a "sunna" or "custom." The Hadith lists Mohammed's presumed thoughts or actions in a specific situation, a type of "code of conduct."

* Narrated Abdullah: Allah's Messenger said, "The blood of a Muslim who confesses that none has the right to be worshiped but Allah and that I am His Messenger, cannot be shed except in three cases: in Qisas (equality in punishment) for murder, a married person who commits illegal sexual intercourse and the one who reverts from Islam (apostate) and leaves the Muslims." *(Al-Bukhari, 9:17)*

* Narrated Ali: "Whenever I tell you a narration from Allah's Apostle, by Allah, I would rather fall down from the sky than ascribe a false statement to him, but if I tell you something between me and you (not a Hadith) then it was indeed a trick (i.e., I may say things just to cheat my enemy). No doubt I heard Allah's Apostle saying,

"During the last days there will appear some young foolish people who will say the best words but their faith will not go beyond their throats (i.e. they will have no faith) and will go out from (leave) their religion as an arrow goes out of the game. So, wherever you find them, kill them, for whoever kills them shall have reward on the Day of Resurrection. *(Al-Bukhari volume 9:64)*

* Narrated Anas bin Malik: Allah's Apostle said, "I have been ordered to fight the people till they say: 'None has the right to be worshiped but Allah.' And if they say so, pray like our prayers, face our Qibla and slaughter as we slaughter, then their blood and property will be sacred to us and we will not interfere with them except legally and their reckoning will be with Allah." *(Al-Bukhari 1:387)*.

* Mohammed said, "I have been ordered to fight with the people till they say, none has the right to be worshiped but Allah." *(Al-Bukhari 4:196)*

* Mohammed also said, "Know that Paradise is under the shades of the swords." *(Al-Bukhari 4:73)*

* Mohammed said, "Whoever changes his Islamic religion, kill him." *(Al-Bukhari 9:57)*

* Mohammed said, "No Muslim should be killed . . . for killing a Kafir (infidel)." *(Al-Bukhari 9:50)*

* Mohammed said to the Jews "The earth belongs to Allah and His Apostle, and I want to expel you from this land (the Arabian Peninsula), so, if anyone owns property, he is permitted to sell it. " *(Al-Bukhari 4:392)*

* Mohammed's last words were: "Turn the pagans (non-Muslims) out of the Arabian Peninsula." *(Al-Bukhari 5:716)*

* Mohammed once was asked: What is the best deed for the Muslim next to believing in Allah and His Apostle? His answer was : "To participate in Jihad in Allah's cause." *(Al Bukhari 1:25)*

* Mohammed was quoted as saying, "I have been ordered to fight with the people till they say, none has the right to be worshiped but Allah." *(Al Bukhari 4:196)*

* Mohammed also said, "The person who participates in Allah's cause and nothing compels him to do so except belief in Allah and His Apostle, will be recompensed by Allah either with a reward or booty (if he survives) or will be admitted to Paradise (if he is killed)." *(Al Bukhari 1:35)*

THE BIBLE AND VIOLENCE

Some Christians defend the Koran and its violent statements by saying, "Well, the Old Testament has many violent statements about killing others"—implying that *our* Book is just like *their* book. I have personally repeatedly heard this statement made—even by pastors, who should know better. These types of statements reveal the depth of biblical-historical ignorance of many Christians.

A course in "Hermeneutics 101" ("hermeneutics" means "science of interpretation") would be of great help. Certainly the Old Testament does have some commands to kill others. No honest Christian can deny that. But what thinking, honest Christian can justify killing their unbelieving neighbors today (using these same Old Testament texts)? None! Why? Because we all know the Old Testament had a very specific function in a pre-Christian ethic.

OLD TESTAMENT INSISTENCE ON SEPARATION

The major message of the Old Testament is "separate," "do not intermingle," "do not intermarry," etc. It is one of separation, even to the point of using the sword in order to stay separate.

Why? Because God wanted the Israelites all to Himself in order to establish Himself in them—away from any contaminating influences of any other pagan religion. (Admittedly, God wasn't particularly politically correct. The Bible even calls Him "jealous.") Thus, God told Abram to leave Ur (present-day Iraq) and go to a land far away (Israel today). And for two thousand years (from Abraham to the beginning of the New Testament), the message was "stay separate!" In order to do that, it was occasionally bloody—not at all to any of our liking. Thus some contend that the Old Testament has its own version of jihad—holy war or "struggle." However, the "ethnic cleansing" required of Joshua by God was a very specific command, limited to a precisely defined geographical region and an equally specific time. In contrast, the Koran's "holy war," according to some of its interpreters, is both timeless and borderless (global).

In most portions of the Old Testament and in all portions of the New Testament, there is no call for use of *literal* swords.

NEW TESTAMENT CALL TO INTERMINGLE

For a long period (Old Testament) God poured Himself into the Israelites—so that they would recognize Him when He came in the flesh (although they never really obeyed Him and remained truly separate). Then God commanded precisely the opposite of "stay separate." He said "Go into all nations!" In effect, He is saying, "Now I have established Myself and My ways in you. You should now be strong enough to stay true to My ways, even though you will no longer be insulated from other cultures. And you now have

Me (God) in the flesh (Jesus), so now you can ethnically and nationally intermingle. In fact, I am commanding you to do exactly that."

Thus, the Great Commission: "Go! Disciple. Preach the Day of the Lord. Heal. Evangelize. Deliver. Set the captives free. Lift up the poor. Instead of being 'separate' (Old Testament) because you were not strong enough, you are now to infiltrate (New Testament) because you are spiritually strong enough. In so doing, you are to carry to everyone the fabulously wonderful news, the Gospel—the Good News!" Notice—and this is key—in the distinctly Christian ethic of the New Testament, the sword is never used to "evangelize." The sword was used briefly, for purposes of keeping a people-group separate in the Old Testament—a pre-Christian ethic—but it is not in the New Testament.

NO KORANIC END TO A "DISPENSATION" OF VIOLENCE

Now contrast that to the Koran. It never states that the violence (kill the "infidels"—Jews and Christians) was for a previous "dispensation," thus it should be stopped. There is nothing close to the analogy of the Old Testament/New Testament distinction, thus the command to kill the infidel has not ended. Nowhere in the Koran does it state that it must be stopped because we are in a "new era."

In fact, the latest writings of the Koran are the most violent—so, the Koran gets more violent—not less so. The Koran, in its late Medina-based texts, calls for death to those who are not Muslim and even more graphically to any person who stops being Muslim.

On September 11, 2001, New York City, Washington, D.C., and Pennsylvania learned what happens when some followers of the Koran took some of those very statements seriously.

More than 3,000 killed! A horrific act! (That number—
3,000—is, by the way, the same number of Christians who
are killed somewhere on the globe every 7 days—160,000
per year, or one every 3 minutes—simply for following Jesus.
Many of those are killed in Muslim countries, due to Muslim
laws, based on the Koran.) To my knowledge, no other *major*
world religion has, as its written corpus, such clarion calls
for the deaths of Jews and Christians.

RETALIATION IS UN-CHRISTLIKE

In spite of Muslims' violence, we do not have the luxury
as Christians to retaliate. In the days following September
11, 2001, some Muslims were harassed and threatened in
the United States. Mosques and Muslims should not be
attacked or harmed. That is repulsive to the Gospel and
harms our Christian witness. The best strategy is for
Christians to love Muslims, reach out to them, develop
quality relationships with them. It is wrong for Muslims to
be harassed in this country. But it is equally wrong for
Christians to be harassed in Muslim countries. And tragically, American Muslim organizations and leaders are silent
regarding the human rights violations—directed at
Christians—that occur daily in Islamic nations.

ISLAM: A RELIGION OF PEACE?

In the days that followed September 11, Muslim clerics,
political pundits, politicians, and liberal preachers repeatedly stated the mantra: "Islam is a religion of peace." If
Islam were truly a religion of peace, then non-Muslims held
captive simply for differing religious beliefs would be
released from Muslim jails, and government officials and

religious leaders would apologize for the Islamic persecution, incarceration, and imprisonment of Christians.

President George W. Bush and Colin Powell have frequently stated that this peace-loving religion (Islam) was simply "hijacked" by fundamentalists. This was said, no doubt, to help stabilized a fragile coalition of nations fighting terrorism in Muslim nations. Surely they must have said that for purely *political* purposes. They certainly could not have meant that *theologically* or *historically.* Theology and history defy that statement.

But many churches in our nation picked up on this presidential decree and echoed it within their walls. There has been a rush to show unity with Muslims from many denominational and independent churches. One United Church of Christ fellowship announced it would substitute readings from the Koran for Bible readings for eight consecutive Sundays. The pastor of one of the nation's largest Methodist churches declared in a magazine article that God is the same one worshiped in "mosques, synagogues, and churches."

Then Franklin Graham, son of well-known evangelist Billy Graham, took a bold and controversial stand. He referred to Islam as "a very evil and wicked religion."[28] He later defended the statement, explaining that he had many Muslim friends, but he still decried evil acts done in the name of Islam.[29]

MUSLIM "PEACE" DEFINED

Whenever there is a dispute (Islam is peaceful/Islam is violent), it is important to know definitions of the words that are being debated, in this case the definition of "peace." George Braswell, who lived in Iran for seven years, helps define "peace" from a Muslim perspective: "The world . . . of

Islam must conquer and rule over those of ignorance and disobedience . . . The peace of the world cannot be secured until
the peoples come under the rule and protection of Islam."[30]
"Peace" to Islam is Muslims controlling all non-Muslims.
Braswell continues,

> All (Author's note: The text states *all,* not *some.)*
> Muslims are under mandate to practice jihad
> because they believe that Islam is the correct and
> perfect religion and that all other religions are infe-
> rior. Not only are they to follow the teaching of the
> Koran, but they are also to emulate the model of their
> prophet Mohammed, who led his fighting forces into
> battle to defend Islam and to make Islam dominant.[31]

When typical Americans think of "peace," they envision
more than the absence of war. Americans think of freedom
of conscience, freedom to make decisions, freedom of movement. To Islam, "peace" is the Muslim *shari'a* law ruling all
humanity. These are two very conflicting definitions of "peace."

"THE MAJORITY OF MUSLIMS ARE . . . "

Repeatedly I have heard persons say, "The majority of
Muslims are peaceful." A "majority" would be approximately
600-700 million. Do we really know whether the *majority*
(50% plus 1) is peaceful or not? It should be noted that there
is a difference between "Muslims" and "Islam." Obviously
many Muslims, *as individuals,* are peaceful and peace loving.
But that is not to say that Islam, *as a religion,* is inherently
peaceful. It is not. At least, not in most countries where
Islam is in the majority—or where it is striving to become the
dominant force.

In a graduate-school class on Islam, I made an observation and asked the following question: "Those who enjoy good relations with Muslims as their neighbors tend to say, 'Most Muslims are peace-loving.' Those who come from Muslim countries with physical scars on their bodies (caused by Muslims) and threats against their lives (because of their Christian faith) tend to say, 'Most Muslims are violent.' But both claims regarding *'most Muslims'* are purely anecdotal. Is there any reputable, statistical study which would reveal if the *majority* of Muslims are, in fact, peace-loving or violent?"

To that, the professor stated that there is no such study. Tragically, however, there is credible evidence that the fastest-growing "wing" of the faith is the Islamists (militant fundamentalists). He concluded: "There is a war going on for the very 'soul' of Islam between the 'moderates' and the 'militant fundamentalists.'"[32] We are told that "militant Islamic fundamentalists, or 'Islamists,' represent a narrow, murderous, fringe." Supposedly, they number no more than 10 percent, at most 15 percent, of all Muslims. Ten percent of 1.2 billion Muslims works out to 120 million people. However, there does not seem to be any credible evidence that actually tells us what the real numbers are.

In radio and television interviews, Muslims constantly insist that Islam is a religion of peace. Samar Hathout articulated the frustration of Muslims being "stereotyped" as violent at a United Nations Women's Conference:

> We are still perceived as foreigners; we are still
> perceived as people out to destroy the United States,
> and when we attempt to define ourselves, our voices
> are silenced. When mainstream Muslims are given
> the rare opportunity to explain Islam, we are told that
> we, as moderate Muslims, are the minority and that

most Muslims are actually violent extremists. This image of Muslims as violent extremists is perpetuated by the media, which chooses to report primarily negative images of Islam and Muslims. This image is further intensified by the profound ignorance of the average American about Muslims and Islam.[33]

I would suggest that this "stereotype" of Islam is not rooted in *our* ignorance, as Hathout stated. It is rooted in *their* history—a long history in which so many Christians (and people of many other religions, as well) have been *and are being* persecuted by Muslims. If Samar Hathout and other moderate Muslims want to assure Christians that Islam is a religion of peace, they need to join voices with ours in calling for the end of religious persecution in the Muslim nations of the world.

In the course of writing this book, I was in a meeting with approximately 120 Christians. Also present was 1 Muslim, the leader I was later told, of some 67 Islamic centers in that particular state. At one point, we had the opportunity to share some thoughts with the rest of the group. The Muslim present was the first one to have access to the microphone. He was poised and gracious. But what he said deeply disturbed me. He rationalized the actions of the Islamic fundamentalists who flew airplanes into the World Trade Center towers by saying that all religions "have a few bad apples." Then, looking at us, he said, "You have your Timothy McVeighs and your Jim Joneses, and we have a few fundamentalists."

I was stunned! What a comparison! And what denial! (The comparison is so feeble and pathetic that I hesitate using space to discuss it.) McVeigh (who is hardly associated with Christianity) and Jones are two bizarre individuals who brought localized destruction, two morbid "bookends," twenty-three years apart. Contemporary Islamists, who number in the tens (hundreds?) of millions, are terrifying dozens of nations and have generated fear in much of the earth for nearly a quarter of a century. McVeigh's and Jones' actions aren't supported by any credible reading of biblical texts. Islamists, in contrast, can point to numerous koranic verses, and to many historical examples from the fourteen hundred years of Muslim heritage, in order to justify their conduct. Had the Muslim that day admitted the pervasiveness of Islamic fundamentalist terror (even though he himself was a "moderate" Muslim), he would have established a "bridge" of trust. His attempt to distortedly "broad brush" history only created further distrust.

James Beverley posed a significant question: "Islam stands at . . . a crossroads since September 11. The tensions it has been facing for centuries have risen to the surface. Is Islam a religion of peace? Does it believe in human rights? Can it find a way to be a part of the human community without violently insisting on its own way?"[34] That is the key question.

EVIDENCE: PEACEFUL OR VIOLENT?

What are some evidences that support the notion that Islam is either a peaceful or violent religion? If, by chance, every single verse from the Koran that speaks of violence has been actually taken out of context, and actually does not mean what it appears to mean (as some suggest), what are other ways to discern whether or not Islam is "a religion of peace?"

THE FOUNDER'S LIFE

First, let's look again at the life of Mohammed. It is not by accident that one of the world's museums displays the sword (or purported sword) of Mohammed. (In contrast, Jesus had no sword that could be displayed.) Mohammed led 66 military campaigns. He attacked caravans and innocent Jewish encampments. Many innocent men, women, and children were slaughtered. In order to determine whether or not "Islam is a religion of peace," it would be good if we were able to ask the people in the seventh-century Quaraysh caravans that question. We should ask the Jews in and around Medina in approximately A.D. 620 that question. We might want to talk to those who were the inhabitants of Mecca in A.D. 622 (the first city overrun by Muslim armies) if Islam is "about peace." Mohammed's followers try to claim that he was only "defending" himself, and certainly there were *some* situations in which this was the case. But there were many more cases in which he attacked. This is hardly a good beginning for a religion of peace.

EARLIEST YEARS AFTER MOHAMMED

Next, let's look at this issue historically, specifically the caliphs (successors) who followed Mohammed. Abu Bakr led armies that forced succeeding tribes to stay under Islamic domination. Umar, the second caliph, was assassinated by a Persian prisoner of war. This particular caliph was known for the Omar covenant which expresses hostility toward Christians and Jews:

> The necks of thimmis (Jews and Christians) are to be sealed when collecting the Jezzieh (tax imposed on Jews and Christians). The method of sealing is to bind the necks of the person with a collar. In it is a piece of lead, stamped with the amount of his payment. The collar is not to be broken until the payment is completed. This is in accordance to the koranic verse 'Until they pay the Jezzieh by an upper hand, may they be subjugated (humiliated)' . . . And if the person was a Jew, he must wear on his shoulder a red or

yellow banner, so he is recognized as a Jew. And if the person is a Christian, he needs to wear harsh clothes, with a large pocket in the chest area like women. As for Christian women, they must wear shoes with different colors, one black and the other white. And if a Jew or a Christian goes into a public bath, he must wear an iron, copper, or lead-made collar around his neck, so he can be identified from Muslims. Never a Jew or a Christian can build houses higher than a Muslim. They are not to crowd public roads but need to use narrow alley ways and small streets. They are not to be saluted, nor can their graves be extended beyond the surface of the ground.[35]

Uthman, the third caliph, was assassinated by a fellow Muslim, as was Ali, the fourth caliph. At that point civil war broke out (A.D. 656-60). This is hardly a religion with a history of peace. During the same period, Muslims murdered one million Christians across northern Africa. Such wholesale slaughter is not the characteristic of a religion of peace.[36]

The Islamic Umayyad Dynasty (as noted in the previous chapter) ruled the vast Muslim Empire from A.D 661 to A.D 750. Another Civil War occurred from 680-692. In 750, the Abbasids established a new dynasty, and in the process, massacred almost every member of the Umayyad family. And this same story could be told repeatedly over hundreds of years. This does not sound like a religion of peace.

MUSLIM GOVERNMENTS

Let's examine a third indicator. If history is not convincing, let's look at governmental structures. There are twenty-two countries in the League of Arab Nations. There are approximately forty nations with a Muslim majority. In which of these nations would non-Muslims want to live as Christians or Jews? Saudi Arabia is a friend of the United States but has been voted the worst persecutor of Christians. Two million Sudanese Christians have been killed by Muslims imposing Islamic law. And the list could go on. Islamic armies and governments during the last fourteen centuries have killed millions of Christians, and many Christians are held and tortured in prisons in Islamic countries even as you read this.

In a book written since September 11, 2001, James Beverley raises the obvious question that so many seemed at first unwilling to ask: "Why do Muslim countries have such deplorable records on human rights?" He continues that discussion in a *Christianity Today* article published in January, 2002:

> Of the 41 countries whose population is at least 70 percent Muslim, 26 are considered not free, and 13 are partly free. Only two are free—meaning they protect political and civil rights as defined by the United Nations Declaration of Human Rights.[37]

Cutting to the chase, he makes a statement and then poses a question: "It would be wonderful to know that the Muslim leaders who joined President Bush in public to express solidarity against Osama bin Laden were already on record as condemning the persecution of these Christians in Afghanistan? If not, why not?"[38] That question still stands.

Most ironic is the reason why many Muslims immigrate from Islamic countries to the U.S., which is supposedly "the great Satan." Like others who come to America, they hope for freedom and opportunities for themselves.

PEACEFUL MUSLIMS

"But what about my Muslim neighbors?" people ask. "They are peaceful. They don't follow any verses in the Koran which say to kill me!" Certainly this is true. The Muslims that I know are peaceful. In fact, those (peaceful ones) are the only kind of Muslims I want to know!

There are many peaceful Muslims. Some Muslims are even unaware of the violent koranic texts. And many certainly don't know the history of Islam. And, if they live in the United States, they may have little awareness of the constant persecution of Christians in Islamic nations.

SECULAR, NOMINAL, MODERATE, AND LIBERAL MUSLIMS

Some Muslims are "secular" Muslims. They are similar to people in America who say they are Christian, but they have no Christian understanding at all. There are certainly counterparts in Islam. These would be called "nominal" Muslims, that is, "in name only." Other Muslims are "moderates." They have some knowledge of the Koran but try to "fit in" to modern life. They downplay the violent koranic texts. Some would be labeled "liberal" Muslims.[39] But, tragically, a growing number of Muslims are "fundamentalists;" and one of the fastest growing groups of "fundamentalists" are "Islamists," or militant Muslims.

The various "strains" or types of Muslims can be "charted" by a *"social* axis"—which covers a spectrum from *radical* (socialistic / militant / revolutionary) on one end to *conservative* (capitalistic / peaceful) on the other end—and a *"religious* axis," with a spectrum extending from *fundamentalist* on one end to *secular* on the other end.

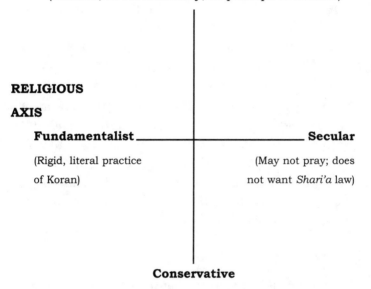

SOCIAL AXIS

Radical

(Militant, or revolutionary, or perhaps socialistic)

RELIGIOUS

AXIS

Fundamentalist   **Secular**

(Rigid, literal practice   (May not pray; does

of Koran)   not want *Shari'a* law)

Conservative

(Capitalistic, peaceful)

Look at the chart for a moment. If a Muslim group is fundamentalist (following a strict interpretation of the Koran) and radical (militant), it would fit into the upper left-hand quadrant. If it is radical (militant) and secular (somewhat non-religious), it would fit into the upper right-hand corner. If it is a group which is fundamentalist (following strict koranic interpretation), yet peaceful, it fits in the lower left-hand corner. And finally, if the Muslim group is secular and peaceful, it is in the lower right-hand quadrant. Certainly there are many "shades" of Muslims in between the four I have described. Admittedly this is simplistic, but it helps one understand the enormous variety within Islam.[40]

CHRIST'S COMMISSION—LOVE MUSLIMS

In the days following September 11, some Muslims were harassed and threatened in the United States. Mosques and Muslims should not be attacked or harmed. That is repulsive to the Gospel and harms our Christian witness. Succinctly stated, Jesus would never "graffiti" a mosque. And, if we know of so-called "Christians" committing such an act, we should repent on their behalf for it being done "in Jesus' name."

The best strategy is for Christians to love Muslims, reach out to them, and develop quality relationships with them. It is wrong for Muslims to be harassed in this country. But it is equally wrong for Christians to be harassed in Muslim countries. And tragically, American Muslim organizations and leaders are silent regarding the human rights violations that occur daily in Islamic nations.

SUMMARY

In summary, let me reiterate that some Muslims are peaceful and peace-loving and base their lives on the Mecca-based (early) portions of the Koran. Some Muslims are violent and base their actions on the Medina (late) portions of the Koran. But Islam, based upon (1) the life of its founder, (2) fourteen hundred years of history, (3) the laws and governments it produces, and (4) its holy writings, is *not* a religion of peace.

Let us pray that the recent militant surges within contemporary Islam dissipate. And pray that "moderate" Muslims are able to become predominant within Islam. And that peace and tolerance towards Christians will prevail within Islamic countries. And that Christians will have the opportunity to be authentic witnesses to Muslims, who will in turn discover the freeing power of the Gospel of Jesus Christ. That is my prayer.

CHAPTER 5

AUTHENTIC CHRISTIANS—
HOW *NOT* TO RELATE TO MUSLIMS

As we begin this chapter, it would do us well to remember what was said in the first chapter: This book is not ultimately about Islam. It is about "a Christian's *response*" to Islam. In this chapter we will talk about how *not* to respond. In chapters 6 and 8, we will discuss *positively* responding to Islam.

Approximately three thousand persons lost their lives on September 11, 2001. But there was one death that was underreported. That death was truth. Truth died on that fateful day. (This is the key to this entire book; this thought is the *reason* for this book.) Media commentaries that followed that horrific day frequently referred to every deceased person as "being in Heaven." Universalism reigned. Most bizarre was Oprah Winfrey's notion that everyone killed in the World Trade Center in New York had become an angel!

It is cruel to lie to people—especially when their eternity is at stake. The days following September 11 were splendid opportunities to examine how to be prepared for the afterlife—making it to Heaven, avoiding Hell. But the "loudest" voices in the post-9-11 responses verbalized the universalistic "everyone-went-to-Heaven" mantra. But what is more tragic is that surveys indicate that most Americans believe some vague version of universalism (the results of "my good works" outweighing "my bad deeds"). And the consequences of believing such an untruth are horrific and lasting.

The one institution that could and should have been in a position to correct such harmful thinking was evangelical Christianity. But is seemed alarmingly impotent. We expect "liberals" to act like liberals. And liberal churches did just that (affirming universalism; telling Muslims we all worship the same "God"). But September 11 was profoundly alarming in that *evangelical* churches started acting like liberals. We (as evangelicals) had a mirror held up to us in the days following that fateful September day, and what we saw defied our rich, Jesus-centered heritage. Evangelicals, for the first time, seemingly denied their former Christo-centricity (Christ centeredness). John 14:6—*"No one comes to the Father except through me* [Jesus]"—had apparently disappeared from many Bibles. If my analysis is right (and I pray I am wrong), something worse than the World Trade Center loss occurred on September 11. *It was the day truth died.* And if the evangelical church does not "step up to the plate," many of America's church buildings, within a half century, will have crescent moons on their steeples rather than crosses. (Lest you scoff, there are several formerly predominantly Christian countries who said, "It will never happen to us." But it did.)

My goal in this chapter (and the next one as well) is a call for the reestablishment of a bona fide Christ-centeredness—Jesus centeredness. One of the goals of this chapter is to reduce the naïve and imprecise thinking that has afflicted so many Christians in relating to Muslims (especially since the September 11, 2001 terrorists attacks in New York City and Washington, D.C.). Understanding the truth about the differences between Islam and Christianity will help us all fine tune our commitment as authentic Jesus followers. I also hope to establish a road between two ditches:

1. Ditch "A" is abuse of Muslims, or "Muslim-bashing;" this certainly is inappropriate.

2. Ditch "B," as I am calling it, is the knee-jerk reaction of platforming Muslims in Christian churches, thus implying that "We all worship the same God" or buying into the politically correct line that "Islam is a religion of peace." This particular ditch is lethal to the truth of the Gospel of Jesus Christ and to Muslims who go to a Christless eternity.

Both ditches are ultimately very *unloving* to Muslims. Somewhere between those ditches is a highway of compassion and ministry to Muslims, whose travelers are informed by a grasp of Christian and Islamic history, an analysis of the Koran, an understanding of Muslim governments and the Islamic agenda, and above all, a clear understanding of Christ's sufficiency on the Cross.

THE INCREASING MUSLIM "PRESENCE" IN AMERICA

In the United States, the growth of Muslims is strong and steady. Already their influence is being felt in our education system. In Byron, California, seventh-grade students are made to dress up as Muslims, read the Koran, and conduct a "holy war" or jihad using a dice game in a state-mandated curriculum which does not offer the same privilege to the Christian faith.[41] The New York City Public Schools administration now allows Muslim children to be excused from classes to go to a state-funded classroom for their daily prayers. Christian children are forbidden to pray or conduct Bible studies in the same schools. In Massachusetts, the governor has expressed interest in introducing Muslim teaching into the state's school curriculum.

I am not advocating Muslim-bashing, nor am I calling for immigration laws to keep Muslims from coming to America. This is, after all, a land of opportunity for all oppressed people. But once again I remind you: Islam, at its core, is not a religion that is satisfied with peaceful *coexistence* with other religions. To be true to the faith, a Muslim must seek—through peaceful or, if necessary, violent means—to exert Islamic influence in all areas of his society. What might this mean in American culture? Specifically, what does this mean to the Church in America? We are ignorant if we think that Muslims are just like us, just a "religion," and that we can all worship side by side. Islam, at its core, does not have such tolerance.

THE INAPPROPRIATENESS OF "PLATFORMING"

Since the terrorist attacks, some Christians pastors have invited Muslims to Christian worship services to be honored and in some cases to be brought to the platform. And if that is not enough, some of the Muslims have been invited to talk to the congregation, even going so far as to offer Islamic prayers in a Christian church! This is certainly in vogue right now in many churches. It seems to be very politically correct. There is a great misunderstanding among (no doubt) well-meaning people as to the message they are sending when a Muslim is invited to sit on the platform during a worship service. Yes, Muslims should be loved, cared for, and prayed for. But when Muslims are platformed in Christian churches, this dilutes the Gospel, perhaps causing those in attendance to question *whether Jesus alone is the source of salvation.*

West End Methodist Church of Nashville invited Ilyas Muhammad, imam at the Muslim American Community

Center, to teach a Sunday school class and lead the group in prayer.[42] Muslim cleric Faisal Hammouda, in one of America's largest evangelical churches (if not *the* largest evangelical church), announced from the platform that "We (Muslims) believe in Jesus, more than you (Christians) do, in fact." According to a news reports, the pastor "ventured to disagree."[43]

When pastors invite Muslims to speak in their churches, do all the people in the audience really understand that Muslims do *not* believe that Jesus died and rose again, the capstone of Christian belief and faith? Although pastors of churches may themselves be thoroughly Christo-centric, their actions (inviting Muslims to speak in a worship service) "beam" a mixed message to the congregation (who are in a culture already saturated with pluralistic thinking): there may be other "roads" to Heaven besides Christ.

As I was writing this chapter, I received a desperately worded e-mail from a former Muslim (now a Christian). He pleaded with me to confront a pastor of a large church who had a Muslim on the platform in the worship services who "blasphemed our Lord." Those were the words used in the desperate e-mail. Why would godly men, who are normally so discerning, chose to platform Muslims in services designed to honor Christ?

No one would dispute that there are appropriate times and places for Christian-Muslim dialogue, but a worship service is *not* one of them. A specially advertised seminar-type venue would seem to be totally appropriate in a church building, so long as the Christian moderator is articulate well versed in the Koran, Islamic ways and history, Muslim governmental policies regarding Christians, and contemporary trends within Islam.

Let me be quick to say that I do not agree with the mistreatment of Muslims that occurred in the days following September 11. Mosques and Muslims should not be attacked. That is repulsive to the Gospel and harms our Christian witness. Succinctly stated, Jesus would never "graffiti" a mosque. It is wrong for Muslims to be harassed in this country. Our God does not call us to a campaign of evangelism that includes violence against nonbelievers.

A DIRECT AND FORCEFUL QUESTION

Allow me to ask a very direct (and unpopular) question: Do the Muslims who are being applauded in Christian churches reject the Koran scriptures that call for the killing of all Jews and Christians? Let me assume that they are "moderates" and consequently do understand these verses to have no application today. Then let me ask a second question: Why are Muslims (if they are, in fact, as peace-loving as some contend) not making a loud outcry against the persecution, torturing, and killing of Christians that has occurred and is occurring in Islamic nations right now? Putting aside *freedom of religion* issues, why aren't peace-loving Muslims demanding an end to such atrocities on a *human rights* basis?

Recently, I took a dozen pastors on my staff to a major Los Angeles mosque. We sat and talked with their leaders there for more than an hour in a very congenial, gracious, and cordial environment. We had a most enjoyable visit and were most appreciative of their hospitality. In a separate meeting with one of the local leaders, I asked forgiveness for atrocities committed by Christians on Muslims through the centuries, specifically during the Crusades—A.D. 1100-1300. (See endnote.)[44] I did not apologize to him in order to "extract" an apology from him. This was simply my first opportunity to ask forgiveness of a Muslim in a position of authority. My apology to him stood on its own and had merit whether or not he ever returned an apology. In other words, my apology was not conditional.

But what happened next was quite interesting: I outlined an abbreviated history of Muslim attacks on Christians. Not only did the Muslim leader *not* apologize, he would *not acknowledge any truth* in what I was saying. He denied historical reality, and that was under the most cordial, gracious, non-combative circumstances. (When I asked a prominent scholar on Islam why Muslims would be "in denial" regarding such well-documented historical realities, he responded: "There is an Eastern principle: 'To have a fault is one fault; if you *admit* it, you have *two* faults.'") And it is a denial I have heard repeated over and over through national media in the days since the September attacks. And apparently, many evangelical pastors must also be in denial, for surely they would not platform (in a *worship service)* persons who were part of a movement that has killed tens of millions of Christians if they (the pastors) were aware that such atrocities actually occurred and are still presently occurring.

MORE PLATFORMING

On Sunday, September 16, 2001, a widely known, nationally televised Southern California pastor had a Muslim cleric on the platform of his church (aired September 23, 2001). The Muslim was given an opportunity to speak to the audience. He addressed the crowd as "my brothers and my sisters."

As I understand the Bible, my brothers and sisters are those who are "in Christ." Are Muslims my brothers or sisters? Certainly they can be my friends; they can be my neighbors; I can reach out to them in love—and I should. But should they be honored (simply because they are Muslim) in the "house" that is set aside for Jesus-worship? No!

That congregation gave the visiting Muslim cleric a standing ovation. Frankly, it was offensive. In my opinion, the applause was based on a "platitudinal love." Platitudinal love is a gentle "let's all get together now and just be nice to everybody" kind of love. A bona fide biblical love says the following: Jehovah God created you; He loves you passionately; we love you; but without Jesus, you will go to a Christless eternity. And we care about you way too much not to tell you about Him. But they (the applauding people) are not to blame. They were set up for it. They did not know. They had no grasp of the dimension of their actions.

As I watched that scene, I had a shuddering thought. What if some Christian who was being tortured in a Muslim jail would have been forced to watch that sight? The American Christians in that Southern California church applauded in ignorance, I believe, not in knowledge.

APPROPRIATE RESPONSE

Now I would have stood and applauded too—if those in attendance that Sunday morning would have been urged by their pastor to do individual acts of kindness, compassion, and Christian witness to their Muslim neighbors. I would have been excited if their leader would have admonished them to "seize this moment" to love Muslims, both in *action* and *word.* By *action* I mean such things as buying groceries for the Muslims if they were afraid to go out to a store for fear of retaliation. By *word,* I mean saying such things as "May I, during these difficult days, tell you why I care for you so much? May I speak with you about Jesus, who He is, and His love for you?" For that, I would have stood and applauded. Why? Because it is good and right and Jesus-honoring! And it *is* Jesus' strategy. (He did not *"platform"* Gentiles in synagogues. He reached across social and ethnic lines and loved them.) Repeating the obvious, we should not "platform" Muslims in what are supposed to be worship services centered on Jesus and clap and cheer for them.

THOSE WE SHOULD APPLAUD

I chose to stand and applaud the hundreds of thousands of Christian believers who have refused to renounce their faith in Christ, even in the face of certain death. I stand and applaud the martyrs through the centuries who would not deny their Christian faith as they watched their wives and daughters being raped and their sons tortured, as their own arms and legs were being cut off. I stand and applaud Jesus followers who have withstood the unspeakable acts done to them by Islamic armies yet would not back down.

I choose to stand with them! They are my heroes! I stand and applaud the martyrs (most of them unknown) of the faith. I do not (in a "Jesus house of worship") stand and applaud persons who are part of a movement which has been responsible for the deaths of so many believers.

I care not that the above is not considered acceptable in contemporary culture. In fact, I am aware that it is not. I would clap for the martyrs (and keep telling their stories) even if I were the last voice and the last pair of hands to clap for them. I cannot and will not applaud those who are part of a movement which has slaughtered, mutilated, raped, tortured, and disfigured my *true* brothers and sisters. Those who do this to my true brothers and sisters are *not* my brothers and sisters. If you doubt my stance, perhaps you should ask the Christians in Muslim jails right now, in many Muslim nations, if they think we should bring Muslims into our Christian worship services and applaud them.

Should we love the Muslim "in Christ?" *Yes!* Find ways to reach out to them? *Yes!* Dialogue with them? *Yes!* Share the Good News with them. *Yes!* Pray for them? *Yes!* Applaud them in our Christian churches? *No!*

ONE LAST GROUP TO APPLAUD

I was recently asked to do a one-hour video of the history of Christianity to be used to train Chinese Christians who are willing to buy one-way tickets to go all over the world, to be "invisible" missionaries. They will support themselves as cab drivers or cleaning persons ("tent-making" jobs), knowing that they may never see their homeland again, determined to take Jesus to countries where no Westerner could ever go. These amazing young believers will live on only one dollar per day, just thirty dollars a month, just so they can share Jesus. They are young, single, and radical—completely sold out for Jesus.

These are the ones I want on my platform. In fact, I am not worthy to introduce them. I need to learn from them, rather than me teaching them! If I could, I would put them all on my platform and applaud and applaud!

CHAPTER 6

JESUS—THE NAME THAT IS ABOVE ALL NAMES

In a previous chapter we looked at how the god of the Muslims is not the same as the Lord God Almighty, the God of Christians and Jews. And we know that while Muslims hold Jesus in high regard as a prophet, they do not acknowledge Him as the Son of God. As a matter of fact, this very idea is offensive to a Muslim. Thus, we see that belief in Jesus and His incarnation, His sinless life, His sacrificial death, and His bodily resurrection is a belief held only by Christians. Seeing Jesus as fully God and yet fully man makes our faith unique. So when Christians shy away from speaking the name of Jesus—for fear of offending some or just for fear—they are denying the very Person who makes their faith valid.

IN JESUS' NAME?

When we are with non-Christians, should we pray "in God's name" rather than "in Jesus' name"? How do we live the Christian faith in a "pluralistic" society? When we are with Muslims (or any other religious group), should we try to "blend in" so as not to offend, and for the purpose of establishing some "common ground"?

I believe that Christians should stop referring simply to "God" so as not to offend but should boldly and unabashedly proclaim the name of Jesus, including praying "in Jesus'

Name"—even in places where non-Christians may be gathered. We don't speak Jesus' name for the purpose of being offensive. We speak His name because *He is Lord*. But in the speaking of His name, some are offended. So be it! Tragically, however, due to living in a pluralistic culture, there is a marked hesitancy to use Jesus' name—the Name of the One who was willing to die for them!

A PRIME EXAMPLE

On Sunday afternoon, September 23, 2001, Yankee Stadium hosted "A Prayer for America" designed to comfort a nation so scarred by the September 11 tragedy. Thousands gathered. Muslims read from the Koran. Hindus prayed. Sikhs prayed. Oprah Winfrey, America's best-known New Age guru, emceed! Bette Middler was a type of "praise leader." Christians were represented by Catholics, Lutherans, Armenians, Eastern Orthodox, and the ecumenical—and blatantly liberal—Council of Churches. All were either "liberal" or "liturgical" in "slant." No problem. Include them!

But, where were the Evangelicals, or Pentecostals, or Charismatics, or anyone of a "conservative" bent? Did someone just happen to overlook them? All of them?

Evangelical and conservative churches are among the largest attended churches in New York City: Jim Cymbala, at Brooklyn Tabernacle with thousands trying to get in every Sunday; A. R. Bernard, at the 5,000 seat Brooklyn Christian Life Centre with 10,000 attending weekly; David Wilkerson, at the Times Square Church with thousands in attendance each week. All of these churches have worship services running continuously *all day* Sunday, due to so many trying to get in. I have been to all of them on more than one occasion. On some Sundays, people have to wait two hours to get in! Where were these great men of God? Were they asked to take part? If not, why not? These men are Jesus centered (like all Christians are supposed to be)! I must conclude by their absence that being a "Jesus" Christian is not "cool," not politically correct.

Here is a clue to the answer to the above question. Listen to this amazing fact: *Jesus' name was barely mentioned at Yankee Stadium.* Tragically, it was *so infrequent* that there was a debate by some whether His name was mentioned at all![45] With eight out of ten Americans saying they are Christians,[46] Jesus' name should have been prominent so that there would not have to be a discussion: "Did we hear His name or not?" His name was shockingly scarce. Why? Because some Christians don't want to offend. And as a result, the "salt has lost its savor!" (Matthew 5:13.) We certainly heard the name Allah—and several other names as well! This failure to mention Jesus represents a colossal dumbing down of our Christian faith.

America is 78 percent Christian (or so current surveys show), yet in the *largest gathering* of its type—at the epicenter of the tragedy (New York City), the mentioning of the name of Jesus was conspicuously absent. We have offended the Father by our unwillingness to openly, unabashedly acknowledge His Son's name.

And why don't we mention His name? Why do we downplay it? Because we (or at least some Christians) want to blend in. We (they) long for respectability more than truth.

ACROSS AMERICA—THE SAME PROBLEM

Let's leave New York City now for a moment and go to the country's heartland: Salina, Kansas, population 45,000. Two thousand people attended a September 2001 memorial service for New York City and Washington, D.C., in Salina's Bicentennial Center. Christian pastors read the Bible, Hindu prayers were sung, a Jewish Kaddish was recited, and two passages were read from the Koran. Salina's official city-run Web site lists sixty-five churches but no Muslim mosque, Jewish synagogue, nor Hindu temple. I contacted a pastor-friend in the city to tell me how many Jews, Muslims, and Hindus there were in Salina. He was unable to find any evidence of any Muslims or Hindus (that he was aware of—having lived there for more than three decades), and he thought there were probably one hundred Jewish residents. The local newspaper said the service reflected "America's melting pot." No, it didn't—at least not in a demographically proportionate manner. And it certainly did not reflect the religion demographics of Salina, Kansas.

On Friday, September 14, 2001, in the wake of the September 11 terrorists attacks, a service was held at the National Cathedral in Washington, D.C. In the opening comments, Hindus and Sikhs were referred to respectfully, along with Christians and others—implying the pluralistic "we-all-worship-the-same-God" motif. One prayer ended with "the God of Abraham and Muhammad and the Father of our Lord Jesus Christ" in one phrase. Nothing about that is Christian. That is Hindu (syncretistic: "Let's just put all our 'gods' together") or Bahai ("Just come in through any 'door'—because all religions serve the same god"). To cut to the chase, our polytheistic prayers won't help us. They are a waste of time and breath. They "feel good" and are so chic—so "hip." But they're ineffectual. That "god" or those "gods" can't act in our behalf, because he/it/she/whatever doesn't exist.

A "CHRISTIAN (?)" HIGH SCHOOL

We are all familiar with the battles regarding prayer in public schools. But look at what is happening in some "Christian" schools. The day following the tragic attacks on our nation, a high school affiliated with a major Christian denomination held an all-school assembly to honor the victims of the attacks and to pray for our nation. Students from various religious and ethnic backgrounds were invited to pray in front of all of the students and faculty. Muslims, Jews, even a Buddhist came forward and prayed from a stage while the audience listened. The shocking aspect of this assembly is that not one Christian was asked to pray. Remember, this is supposed to be a Christian-based school, yet no one who confessed Christ as Savior was asked to pray to the only God who lives!

We act as if we are a "Muslim/Hindu/Jewish/Christian/Sikh/Buddhist/etc. nation" *with equal representation* required at any public prayer service. Some Muslims have been quite outspoken that they desire Americans to not speak merely of "a Christian heritage" or "a Judeo-Christian heritage" but rather of "a Judeo-Christian-Islamic heritage!" The most bizarre example of such thinking was recently demonstrated by a decision made by Clarence Wood, Chicago's human-relations commissioner, regarding a Christmas display in Daley Plaza. He required that a repro-duction of a minaret (the tower used to sound calls to prayer to follower's of Islam) be included next to a (Jewish) menorah and a (Christian) nativity scene. Wood said the aftermath of the 9-11 attacks made it even more important that the city government educate its citizens about Islam![47] Since when is it the duty of the city government of Chicago to educate regarding Islam?

The facts are, 78 percent of the people in American at least *claim* they are Christian. Two percent say they are Jewish. Approximately 2 percent say they are Muslim. One third of 1 percent are Hindu. A smaller percentage are Sikhs. With eight out of ten Americans saying they are Christian, we give *equal* billing to every other imaginable religion and yet, on top of that, *rarely mention the name of Jesus*—the Person whom 78 percent of Americans at least *say* they follow.

HIS NAME—*IN ABSENTIA*

Even the word "God" (let alone "Jesus") seemed strangely absent from much of Hollywood's two-hour, multi-network fund raising/"memorial service" on Friday night, September 21, 2001. One actor, quoting the "one nation under God, indivisible" portion of the Pledge of Allegiance, left out "under God." Conspicuously inappropriate (due to the open tears and fervent prayers of the nation) was John Lennon's song "Imagine," sung that night in a haunting rendition by Neil Young, telling us to imagine how wonderful it would be if there were no religion. And blatantly offensive to so many of the families of the three thousand persons who had lost loved ones was the admonition to "imagine" if there were no Heaven.

IN JESUS' NAME

When I am asked to pray at "public" events now, I sometimes receive notes from the person presiding, informing me, in ever-so-subtle terms, to pray "in *God's* name." The implication? Don't use the name of Jesus. I remind those who send me such notes that if I were to demand that a Jewish rabbi or a Muslim cleric could *not* pray a certain way—or if I demanded that they pray "in the name of Jesus"—that would be "intolerant" in our pluralistic culture. They agree with me. Then I remind them that it would be equally "intolerant" for them to demand that I pray a certain way in our pluralistic culture. And they, hesitatingly—knowing their logic has trapped them—agree.

The reason I feel so strongly about praying in Jesus' name is that on one occasion (which I would rather forget), I was asked by the emcee of an event if I would please not mention "Jesus" in my prayer. Caught off guard (which is certainly a pathetically weak excuse), I agreed. I prayed. Honoring the request, I did not pray "in Jesus name." As I walked away from the podium, I felt spiritually contaminated—as spiritually impotent as I have ever felt. In my heart, I cried out, "Oh, Jesus, forgive me for what I have just done! I will never, ever again agree to leave out Your name. I don't want You to forget *my* name. I will never again leave out *Yours!*"

I agree with Polycarp, who in A.D. 155, was asked to deny Jesus, so they would not have to burn him at the stake. He said, in effect, "For eighty-six years Jesus has not denied me; why should I deny Him now?"

Several years ago, (while pastoring in another city), we flew a flag from our church's 70-foot flagpole (which was seen by 120,000 people per day traveling on the freeway). It wasn't an American flag, although I am unabashedly patriotic. It was a 25' by 15' "JESUS" flag, comprised of huge, red block letters (all capitals) on a solid white background. John Vaughn, director of the International MegaChurch Research Center, who may know more about churches around the globe than anyone else, visited our church and complimented us for the flag. He then said to me, "I have never seen this done anywhere in the world. You could have put the word 'God' on the flag, and you would not have been criticized. But you have chosen to put the name 'JESUS' on it, so beware of what is ahead."

His name—so controversial, isn't it? So much so that even those who *call* themselves Christian will avoid His name so as not to "offend."

I will close with several questions:

* Are we straightforwardly and unabashedly going to mention the name of Jesus, or will we use the much less offensive term "God," thus "fitting into" all religions?

* If we use the name of "Jesus," aren't we implying that "Allah" and "Yahweh" ("Jehovah" of the Bible) are not the same (remember, the Islamic Allah does *not* have a son), therefore one of them is the *real* God—and the other is *not?* And if so, which one is the real God?

* And if Allah (or other gods of other religions) are not the same as our God (Yahweh in the Bible), why are we worshiping *with* Muslims, or Hindus, or Buddhists, or Sikhs?

Here is the bottom line question: Is Allah the same as Yahweh? Answer: No.

Fortunately, there are still some Christians who aren't afraid to make waves. In January 2001, Kirbyjon Caldwell, pastor of Windsor Village Methodist Church in Houston, prayed at President George W. Bush's inauguration. Pastor Caldwell drew criticism from non-Christians for praying his benediction "in the name that's above all other names, Jesus the Christ. Let all who agree say amen."

I wholeheartedly agree.

CHAPTER 7

AFTER SEPTEMBER 11—ANSWERS TO QUESTIONS

On September 11, 2001, we were a nation in intense grief and shock. And in the midst of that grief, we found ourselves wrestling with questions—many questions—that we were not asking prior to that day. Following are only a few of the questions that we began to struggle with, which demonstrated how our individual "worlds" had changed:

1. ***Why do I feel the way I do?*** The days following the terrorist attacks created in us a healthy "clingy-ness." Nearly everyone I talked to placed long-distance calls to family members simply because we had a need to be with each other. My wife and I immediately called our two grown children, just to hear their voices. Our two youngest children "clung" close to us in the home. We tended to all stay in the same room of the house. This "clingy-ness" in the midst of tragedy is a good, healthy response. It comforts us. Yet, even with the constant "clustering," we still felt deep anguish. Why? Anguish is a form of caring. God made us with the capacity to love, and with that capacity to love comes the corresponding pain of loss—and grief. And on days like September 11 we grieve. The loss of energy, the glassy look in our eyes and other symptoms are normal reactions to tragic loss. God made us with this capacity—the capacity to feel loss.

2. **What shall we as Christians do in times of tragedies such as this?** We are people of action . . . but our primary "action" (as followers of Christ) in a time such as this is prayer. And what do I mean by prayer? I do not mean incessant talking to God but rather listening to Him. In moments that "rock" our world, we need to ask, "God, what are You saying to me? To us? God, what are You doing? Where is Your 'hand' in this catastrophe? In jolting times, as well as normal times, we must turn prayer into a listening experience as much as a talking experience.

3. **How can people be so wicked as to take innocent life?** Actually, this is one of the few easy questions with an equally simple answer. Let's be quite clear: *wicked people do wicked things.* That's why they're called wicked. Don't expect righteous acts from wicked people. Now one may ask, "How could people become so wicked?" We live in a world of both good and evil. From the inception of this planet, humanity has had choices. You and I can choose to follow "right," or we can choose to follow "wrong." Righteousness is a matter of choice. And so is evil. All of biblical history (and the nearly two thousand years of postbiblical history) indicates that there have always been persons who have chosen the path of evildoing. Not surprisingly, wicked people do wicked acts.

4. **What are some of the things I need to be aware of in painful and distressing moments such as this?** First, God loves our cities. Cities are places of unparalleled opportunity. But they are also places of deep wounding. Pray for them. Don't merely see cities as a place for economic opportunity or pleasure or

sports or culture or entertainment. See them as enormous collections of humanity about whom God cares very deeply and over whom Jesus openly cried. Luke 19:41 says simply, "As he approached Jerusalem and saw the city, he wept over it." What do you do when you see your city?

Second, in the midst of this crisis, watch for the "hand of God" in unexpected places. Listen to the stories—many stories, maybe hundreds of them—of miracles, of unexplainable accounts of God's supernatural intervention. Following September 11 we heard unusual reports, such as the one that came from Pastor A. R. Bernard of Christian Life Centre in Brooklyn, a church with 13,000 members. Of the 150 persons from their congregation who work in or around the former World Trade Center area, an amazing 85 percent of them were inexplicably late to, or absent from, work that day. They have no natural explanation as to why that occurred. And almost all of the remaining 15 percent successfully exited the two towers. Listen closely for these stories—stories of the "hand of God."

Third, know that the hundreds of thousands of acts of kindness that are occurring in New York, Washington, D.C., and around American are not from *human* nature. It is the stamp of the *image of God* on the human spirit, a "stamp" that is still visible in even the unregenerate. Sometimes people act more like God than they act like themselves! It is the evidence that Genesis 1:26 is true, that humanity is made in *His* image—and that image will, on occasion, manifest itself even in those who don't truly know Him personally, in the way He would like to be known. This "image" is simply another evidence of His omnipotence and His love, His "mark" on us all—from Creation.

Fourth, let's not miss the obvious: the September 11 attacks were aimed at three epicenters of our national life: *economic* (the World Trade Center and the financial district), *military* (the Pentagon), and *government* (alleged targets of the White House or the Capitol). They destroyed the first, badly crippled the second, and, for the first time since the presidency of James Madison actually had our president "on the run."

The message here is simple and direct: the foundations of this world are shakable. Only God is *un*shakable. Our *ultimate* confidence can only be in Him. Psalm 20 states that some may boast in "horses and chariots" (military strength), but we must boast in the name of the Lord. Some have said that America is post-Christian ("post-Christian" meaning that Christianity's influence on America has essentially ended). Hopefully this is not the case. But this I do know. Christianity will be post-American. By that I mean simply this: America, as wonderful as it is, will not always be. The kingdom of God will always be and will outlast all nations and empires, including our own.

5. *September 11 spawned a war. Can I support war and still be a follower of Christ? And, due to the way terrorists fight a war (cowardly, hidden among civilian populations), what about innocent persons (including women and children) who die? How can we possibly support a war in*

which that occurs? On occasion, war is the correct course of action. Our past lack of resolve (as a nation) is precisely what has led us into the "9-11" calamity. Failure to act leads to increasingly *more* acts of random, massive terrorism—not only in America but worldwide. And yes, Christians *can* support their nation in war. While we respect those who are pacifists, we believe their position is naïve regarding the profound depths of original sin and to its containment and naïve regarding the authority that God grants to the civil authority to deal with those who disrupt and harm society. War is an acknowledgment that original sin *does* exist—and that, at times, unusual steps must be taken in order to deal with the "collective impact" of original sin manifested in, among other things, terrorists.

It is important to remember that God established three forms of government (family, civil, and church), each with their own powers and limitations. The power to take life is granted to the civil government (to be used in rare cases), not to family government or to church government. And, regretfully, there are times when the civil government must exercise that right. As Dr. Graham Walker, political science professor at The Catholic University of America (Washington, D.C.) stated: "To not exercise that authority would make culpable those in positions of leadership, for the blood of more innocent persons would, in fact, be 'on their hands.'"[48]

And finally, regarding the last question, "Will some innocent women and children die in war?" the answer is a definite yes. In actuality, innocent persons are dying—and did die—in New York,

Washington, D.C., and other places. The precise theological explanation is a concise one: Evil is always
social—it affects far more than the sinners themselves. Sin is always *corporate*. ("Corporate" means
that it impacts many other people, not just the one
"doing the act of sin.") That is why it is always wrong
to say that a sin is a "solo" act. For example, some
say that a man going to a prostitute is a "victimless"
crime. They are wrong. There are many victims:
himself (he has denied his intrinsic value and appropriate expression of his sexuality), the prostitute
(who has devalued herself), and the man's wife or
future wife (as she has lost a bit of the innocent and
beautiful sexual expression that they could have
enjoyed). The loss of trust between the man and wife
will eventually affect the relationship in such a way
that children pay the price of conflict, or separation,
and, in many cases, divorce. The children feel
rejected and wounded in a way that affects them
their entire lives—which is carried to future generations. And yet, some would have the audacity to say
that prostitution is a "victimless" crime? Not so! And
what is true in the above illustration is true in all of
life—especially in war.

War is ultimately the result of sin. And *all* sin is
"corporate" or "social" in its ramifications. The result:
enormous numbers of innocent persons are harmed,
injured, or even killed by war. When the Japanese
bombed Pearl Harbor in 1941, they could not have
imagined that every child in two large Japanese
cities would someday die as a result of the first
atomic bombs. But they did, because "actions have
consequences," and that includes *sinful* actions as

well. Bottom line: a sinful act always hurts more than simply the person doing the sinful act. Like the concentric circles created by a pebble thrown into a pond, the "rippling out" impact wounds many innocent persons around the persons committing the sin.

6. **But aren't we just to "turn the other cheek" as believers? We aren't supposed to retaliate, are we?** Legitimate war is *not* primarily about "anger" and our need to retaliate. It is *not* primarily about the past (bombings, World Trade Center, Pentagon). It is about the future—preventing future genocide and returning us to tranquility and peace—as a nation and as a world. God values justice. The "John 3:16 of the Old Testament" is Micah 6:8, which states: "What does the LORD require of you. To act justly and to love mercy and to walk humbly with your God." Justice, (true) love, and humility are not incongruous. It is right to pray for justice, not out of vengeance (which is the Lord's) but out of the desire for an orderly society (which is God's plan for culture). Justice is another way of saying that people are responsible for what they do, and, in most cases, action needs to be taken to prevent them from doing it again.

7. **But I become afraid when our nation "gears up" for war. What do I do about that?** It is quite normal to be concerned when there are discussions of war. To not be concerned would be abnormal. But, the people of God have survived every war for the past six thousand years—and the Church will survive any future war. And individual believers who do not survive will be swept into eternal reward, for we are not as "those who have not hope" (1 Thessalonians 4:13 TEV). Wars

are, by definition, characterized by casualties. Wise is the person who values life today, lives like it—and, at the same time, is prepared to meet God by receiving Jesus Christ as Savior and Lord.

8. **Were the terrorist attacks of September 11 God's judgment on us?** Well, it certainly isn't a blessing. I'm not sure if this is a judgment or not, but it is a wake-up call, and let's not miss that. Some do refer to it as "judgment" from God—directed to all Americans. They quote Revelation 18:9-20 which speaks of the great city burning, twice mentioning it was destroyed in one hour, and economic activity coming to a halt. I am not sure what to make of this Scripture (whether it has relevance to contemporary times or not). "Judgment" is usually not directly from God but is the consequences of our own disobedience. Jim Cymbala, pastor of Brooklyn Tabernacle, correctly noted that our energy should not go into figuring out whether this is judgment or not but rather into discerning how to make Christ known in the midst of this tragedy. One thing I do know is that this certainly is a spiritual reality check.

So how do we respond to it? *From* what are we waking up (leaving), and *to* what are we waking (personally embracing)? If we cannot answer these questions, we have (tragically) missed the purpose for the "wake up." Wake up *from* lethargy, apathy, and sin. Wake up *to* spiritual vibrancy, deep commitment, and passion for Christ. The most profound verse still remains 2 Chronicles 7:14, "If my people, who are called by my name, will humble themselves and pray and seek my face, and turn from their wicked ways, then will I hear from Heaven and will forgive their sin and will heal their land." It just can't be stated more succinctly than that.

One of the most encouraging "post-9-11" events was a prayer service in our nation's capital on Tuesday evening, December 3, 2001. More than 130 members of Congress, a quarter of the 535 men and women elected to serve in the U.S. Senate and House of Representatives, participated in a voluntary, members only "solemn assembly" held in the Capitol Rotunda. H.C.R. 184, introduced by House Majority Whip Tom DeLay (R-TX) and championed in the Senate by Senator Sam Brownback (R-KS), established the "Day of Reconciliation." The measure set aside congressional business so Senate and House members could privately and voluntarily "gather to humbly seek the blessings of Providence for forgiveness, reconciliation, unity, and charity for all people of the United States . . . "[49]

9. *But aren't the evil terrorists of September 11 "devils"? Why would God allow them to warn us or give us the "wake-up call?"* God used the Assyrians (unbelievers) to address Israel's sins. At the risk of offending, let it not be lost that the radical Muslims who would destroy us, in fact, have *some* morals that we lack. Their accusations regarding us are accurate. They see us as the "devil," in part because we have exported pornography all over the world, because we advocate alcohol usage that has resulted in widespread moral damage, that our movies and entertainment advocate adultery and fornication, and that we kill preborn babies! (The most repulsive response to the tragedy of September

11 was that of Planned Parenthood. They offered free abortions to New Yorkers in the days following September 11. Imagine, after three thousand were killed, Planned Parenthood offers to kill more—for free!)[50] Are we in a position to deny any of the above charges? While it may be ironic that these self-appointed "moralists" can kill unconscionably, let us not forget that they correctly identify issues of wickedness in us.

10. **Are you saying that America "deserved" the terrorist attacks due to our wickedness?** No. Any so-called "deserved" judgment is God's call, not mine. But while we acknowledge America's sins, it is important to be reminded of all that is good, right, and wonderful about America. It has been the greatest carrier of the Gospel. It has stood for truth. America truly has been a bastion of righteousness in so many ways. Beware of so-called "multiculturalism," which is a subtle attack on the values of Western Civilization, specifically Christianity. Beware of "globalism," which is a not-so-subtle way of destroying our national freedoms and bringing us into worldwide tyranny.

Don't be embarrassed by "nationalism." Admittedly, "nationalism" is inappropriate if it is a form of elitism—not valuing others and their cultures. But "nationalism" is good if it means being thankful for the richness of our heritage, the foundations of Christianity that formed this nation, and an appreciation for the unique democracy we enjoy with its accompanying freedoms. There is no need to apologize for America. Her sins have been obvious, and we have apologized and asked forgiveness (for racism and slavery, for example). There are national sins for which we have not yet properly apologized and repented (abortion, for one; the attack upon legitimate marriage by validating same-sex relationships would be another example; hedonism; materialism), and we (or at least some of us) acknowledge that there is sin for which we must repent. But there is much good and righteousness in America, and for that we can thank God for our country.

11. **But in moments of national and global crisis, I'm scared! What do I do?** Although we face difficult and uncertain moments, we are *not* people of fear. Yes, we are occasionally frightened. But, we refuse to "live in fear." We are confident in our God. And we go forward in boldness and deep-seated peace because of Him. Remember that 2 Timothy 1:7 states *God has not given us a spirit of fear, but of power and of love and of a soundmind* (NKJV). It doesn't get any better than that! In turbulent and chaotic times, fear is natural. But we choose not to live in the "natural." We live in the supernatural!

12. **So what should I do or know in times of national and global crisis?** First and foremost, make certain that you know God—*personally*. You can by inviting Jesus Christ into your life to forgive your sins and by making Him the Lord of your life. Do not go through one more moment without that assurance. None of us has the guarantee of another day of life—another second of life. The workers at the World Trade Center on September 11 had no idea that this was their last moment on earth. Undoubtedly, many were ready to meet their Maker. Tragically, some may not have been! If you already

know Christ personally, make certain that you are precisely where God wants you to be. Repent of sin. Renew your commitments. Pastor Jim Cymbala has stated that "less than two dozen men who were willing to die for their cause brought the world's superpower to its knees. Their complete abandonment of their personal agendas—even their lives—is why they have succeeded in doing what they have done. Why do the devil's followers have more commitment than God's?" Walk close to God. Love His children—your brothers and sisters in Christ. Value the Church and her worship services and ministry opportunities. Put a premium on relationships. Stay at the "foot of the Cross." Finally, as followers of Christ, this is "our moment." God put us *here*—at this place, *now*—at this time. *This is our moment!* Savor it!

CHAPTER 8

AUTHENTIC CHRISTIANS—
COMPASSIONATELY RELATING TO MUSLIMS

In previous chapters, we have looked at the reasons why we should not have Muslims seated on our church platforms during worship services, introducing them as our "brothers" and allowing them to lead the congregation in prayer. We have seen that the Islamic Allah is quite different, in character and "content," from Jehovah, the God of the Bible. And we have understood that, in spite of all we are hearing in the news and despite the fact that most of us have friends who are Muslims, Islam, at its core, *as a religion,* is not peaceful.

With this as our foundation, let's examine how to build historically informed and biblically honoring relationships with Muslims at places of work, in our neighborhoods, in our schools. How do we do that? If we really believe John 14:6 (that no one comes to the Father, except through Christ), then we will be diligent to learn how to share Truth (Jesus said He was the Truth, John 14:6) with Muslims in a compassionate, compelling, tender, respectful, winsome, and loving way.

REALLY LOVING MUSLIMS

Here is the key point of this chapter: to *neglect to* lovingly share the Gospel with our Muslim friends is to demonstrate that we are really not willing to treat them as friends.

What kind of persons would *not* share lifesaving information with their friend. What kind of friends are we (to Muslims and other non-Christians) if we just "try to be nice" (such as platforming them) but do not articulate in creative and meaningful ways the pathway to eternal life? The title of this chapter could have been "How to *Really* Love a Muslim." To *neglect to* show someone the way to abundant life is to *refuse to* love them. Clapping for Muslims on the platforms of our churches sounds so good—so vanguard! But it is lethal. It has two results: (1) it lulls us into complacency; and (2) it affirms them in their Christless, works-centered attempt to reach Heaven. God wants something quite different from us. Compassionately sharing Christ with them (in actions and in words) will make a difference one million years from now—in the destiny of every responsive Muslim.

I hope that the next few pages will stir your heart. I hope your heart will be broken for the 1.4 billion Muslims who have the potential of entering a Christless eternity. I once read a haunting magazine article entitled: "Who Weeps for Hagar's Children?" Hagar, of course is the servant girl/"wife" of Abraham who became Ishmael's mother. "Hagar's Children" refers to Muslims. Borrowing that magazine article title (based on Genesis 21:16), I ask you: Will you weep for Hagar's children?[51] Will you weep for Muslims?

HOW TO SHARE

To assist us in the process of learning how to effectively share the Good News of Jesus' resurrection power with Muslims, I asked for help from five experts in developing relationships with Muslims. Four of the five are Middle Easterners. Two are former Muslims (what are referred to as MBBs—"Muslim Background Believers"). The two other

Middle Easterners grew up around Christianity yet have a first-hand, thorough understanding of Islam and the Koran, with the ability to read it in Arabic. The final expert is an American who is passionate about Christ and compassionate towards Muslims.

NASR SADIK

Nasr Sadik wrote the following Muslim "witnessing guideline." Nasr was born and reared in the Middle East. He knows the horror of being persecuted by Muslims for being a Christian—and lives with the implications of that everyday. Consequently he is using a pseudonym here—Nasr Sadik not being his real name. Yet, he has an intense love for Muslims, a desire to see them learn the awesome spiritual freedom that is available through Christ. Here are his thoughts, framed around twenty-seven guidelines.

1. Friendship is first. Invite him/her to your home and show hospitality.

2. Visit their homes, eat with them, and eat their food.

3. Ask the wife to teach you how to cook an authentic meal.

4. Try to understand the Eastern culture:

   a. Dress modestly.

   b. It is important to reach out to the same sex or gender to keep the message clear. In the Eastern culture, most friendships are between persons of the same gender.

   c. Women should speak to the wife away from her husband.

   d. Show respect for the Bible. Don't place it on the floor or in the bathroom. Muslims still consider it the Word of God, even if they haven't read it.

5. Do not give information about a witnessing "strategy." They need to see that you are interested in knowing them as individuals.

6. Do not take this book or any other materials that talk about Islam with you on your visit.

7. Talk to one person at a time. Muslims usually are afraid of each other. Also, news might reach their families.

8. Listen to their problems; offer to pray for them. If possible, pray right away with your friend.

9. Most Muslims have not read or seen a Bible. Giving the Gospel of John is a great idea; it is easy to read and understand.

10. Share your testimony: how you received Christ, what He did for you, the peace that came into your heart.

11. Share the nature and character of God: love, joy, peace . . . etc.

12. Muslims are controlled by fear. They are afraid of their leaders, family, and Allah's judgment on them if they try to read the Bible or discuss other religions, especially Christianity. Sharing God's love for them is important. "Perfect love casts out fear (1 John 4:18 NKJV)."

13. Try to stay away from discussing the Trinity in the first few visits. It is a confusing issue to the Muslims.

14. Present the love of God and the assurance of entering Heaven. Muslims do not have the assurance that after fulfilling the Islamic teaching, they will enter into Paradise. Bring hope to your friend.

15. Stay away from politics, especially the Palestinian-Israeli issue.

16. Insist that the Bible has not been altered or changed. It is the Word of God.

17. Understand a little about the Koran.

18. Continue the relationship; be patient. It takes about a year for a Muslim to make a decision. He or she has to think about the consequences of becoming a Christian.

19. Center your witness on Jesus.

20. Do not underestimate the power of prayer and the power of the Word of God.

21. Do not share a lot from the Koran. The average Muslim doesn't know the Koran and will feel embarrassed.

22. When friendship is established, present the meaning of the death of Christ and the need for the Cross.

23. Ministering to women is very vital; they are lonely and confused. They know that they are not respected by the teaching of Islam, nor do they have any position. They need comfort, and they can only be won through sharing with them in their suffering with love and tears.

24. Women in general are involved in bringing up their children, so it is important to work with the mother to bring her to the knowledge of Christ, for she will influence her children.

25. When sharing with women, present their position in Christ, how Jesus and the Bible respects women.

26. Muslims are generally superstitious, dealing with witchcraft, fortune-telling, and charms to protect themselves from evil spirits. You need to surround yourself with much prayer. It is advisable to work

with intercessors so that you will be covered with prayer before and after witnessing.

27. Respect their dreams; most of the converted Muslims have seen Christ in a dream or a vision. It usually takes supernatural revelation to bring them out of Islam.

ZECHARIA ANANI

Zecharia Anani was raised as a Muslim, then converted to Christianity. He quickly found out the cost of serving Christ after being attacked on numerous occasions. He bears on his body twenty-one different observable wounds. Eleven are from the ravages of war as he fought for Islam in the streets of Beruit, Lebanon. Muslims inflicted the remaining ten following his conversion to Christ. He has been shot, stabbed, beaten, and impaled. Two of his three daughters (the youngest is ten at the time of the writing of this book) have physical scars on their bodies—in some cases on their faces— as reminders that serving Christ costs. After being nearly killed by five men on a street corner, the Christian church he attended felt he must leave the country for the sake of his life. He came to the U.S., then went to Canada. His family was able to join him approximately one and a half years before the writing of this book.

In spite of these painful realities, Zecharia cares deeply about Muslims and does not want to see a single one of them go into a "Christless eternity." Here is his wisdom on sharing Christ with Muslims.

1. As of today, there are more than a billion Muslims who have not received the salvation of Christ nor His good tidings.

2. The Muslim lands and states spread, starting from the shores of Morocco on the Atlantic Ocean, up to the Malaysia Islands and Indonesia, and from Central Asian mountains in China to the Sahara Desert in Africa.

3. Statistics say that there is only one missionary to every million Muslims, and unfortunately, most of them are not qualified enough for this task. And the sad part of the story is that our history is jammed with wars and pettiness which extended for long ages and decades between Christians (some true to their faith and some not) and Muslims at every level and race, place, tradition, and civilization.

4. Our question now: "Is there any possible way that would allow us to cross this very hard and difficult bridge toward the Muslims, so we can convey to them the good tidings of Christ's salvation in a more effective way? Is there a truthful, perfect, and complete way that would make this task possible and easy?"

There is reason to have hope.

MUSLIMS ARE HERE

Remember Muslims and Islam are not far behind seas and mountains or deserts. There is no more need to prepare for years before you go to them—to their land, where you would be ignorant of their social, educational, and traditional life—and to come back after years empty-handed. The Muslims are here today on your streets, in front of your doors, at your schools and universities.

THE HURDLES CAN BE OVERCOME

Reaching out to Muslims here and now is much easier than before and elsewhere. Now Christians are capable of reaching out to them on their own ground and eventually, one on one, at all levels and on all subjects. As a worker in Christ's field, you should be ready with faith and knowledge. Yet there is potential for failure when we witness to Muslims. Here are some of the main reasons:

1. The language obstacle. There are some words, definitions and concepts that are difficult to translate from the koranic Arabic to any other language, which can hinder understanding and communication.

2. The social/cultural challenge. What you regard as normal may be very unusual to persons from a different culture. The Muslim may see things in a very different way.

3. These cultural differences will impact spiritual understanding, causing agreement to be more difficult to attain.

4. The educational gap may negatively impact your ability to witness.

5. And this is the most common reason for failure in witnessing to Muslims: lack of knowledge. You must know the Muslim. Very few have this knowledge, and without it, we will never finish the task.

STEPS FOR SHARING WITH MUSLIMS

How can you reach out to Muslims if you know nothing about them? Who are they? What are they like? How do they think? What do they think? What might insult them? What would they be able to agree with? What will they not accept?

This can be a "high mountain to climb," but here are some points which should help us climb that mountain:

1. Before you begin, be sure you are called by God to serve among Muslims.

2. Be brave. You have to know that your life is in danger. To Muslims, you are an infidel. Their duty is either to make you Muslim or to overcome you.

3. Be patient and strong. Islam has a twisted image of Christianity. The Muslims might appear to agree with you on a lot of subjects and doctrines such as God, angels, the "Holy Book," Hell and Heaven. But, in reality, they do not really agree with you. Patiently, take the time to explain the difference.

4. Be sensitive. You may be at a higher level than they are educationally or socially. Treat them with kindness and patience, like Christ did with all people.

5. Be flexible. Show the Muslims you are truthful with your "friendship" (but don't refer to them as brothers or sisters). Listen to them. Help them. (But do not help them financially unless the Holy Spirit places that on your heart).

6. Be courageous with your witnessing. Convey to the Muslims, no matter how highly educated they are, the simple normal salvation story. The Word of God is the sharpest weapon in your hand, and what extra knowledge you have (on Islam) would be a tool in your hand to defend the faith. Share your own testimony with them. Give them pamphlets, booklets, a New Testament.

7. Be very knowledgeable regarding Islam. You need to at least know the basics of the religion, the history of

Islam, the traditions of Muslims and their social background. This will help you have a strategy, which will get you closer to your friend's heart and make you more effective in winning the Muslim to Christ. When you show that you are familiar with their heritage, your friend will say, "This person is genuine. He knows what even I don't know." Then instead of ignoring you or agreeing with you while you are there and disregarding you when you leave, your Muslim friend will actually listen. Example: When you talk with any Muslim about the Trinity, they may either agree or disagree with you. But as soon as you go, they will say you are a false and ignorant believer and that they have the real truth. But if you show them that you know, by using his doctrine and books, then he will be willing to listen and to welcome you time after time until either you win them to Christ or depart as a friend.

7. Be persistent. When Muslims start listening to you, they won't really be listening to you. They won't get close to you at first. It will take several times, days, weeks, months before either they come to the Lord or they go away. Pursue them once, twice, three times, and more. Help them. Encourage them. Read with them. Read for them. Maybe the tenth time would be the time when the harvest is ripe.

WHEN A MUSLIM ACCEPTS CHRIST

When you go to the harvest, the Lord will grant you the fruit of your work. You will ask yourself then, "What will I do with this new baby in the Lord?" Remember they are totally different. Here are some tips of experience.

1. Give them privacy to confess Christ. When the Muslim is ready to give their soul, heart, and mind to Christ, they will look around to be sure there are no other Muslims around, then they will make the commitment. Now they will be afraid, worried, and ashamed. They are going to insult their family, society, country, and religion. They are going to destroy everything they knew and lived for up until now—destroying all the bridges, putting their life in ultimate danger. They will likely receive death threats for what they are about to do. Don't be hasty and, like some others, unwisely push them to publicly announce their faith prematurely. You might lose your influence with them. Give them time until they are ready. On their own terms, and with time, they will stand tall. For their faith is like a city on a hill. You will be proud of them till the end of life.

2. Now that your friend is an M.B.B. (Muslim background believer), teach them, disciple them, and immediately start studying the Bible with them. Teach them how to pray. Start with the Lord's Prayer. It is a new world for them. Explain things to them, and they will accept and understand.

3. Plant them in a church. Although you are your friend's spiritual parent, you are a tool in the Lord's hand, a bridge for the Muslim to cross to the house of the Lord (the church). Your friend needs a family, attention, and love to grow.

4. Be beside your friend during hard times. The M.B.B. especially during the first couple of years, will face persecution, depression, and sad times. Stand beside them. Even when they are already a member

of a church, help guide and support them. God will bless you more and more.

5. Finally, don't forget your friend. Our Heavenly Father, along the road, will give you more fruit, more spiritual sons and daughters. He might lead you to other fields. You will be busy. The M.B.B. also could become a giant soul winner like you. Time and distance may separate you. But don't forget your friend. Stay in touch with them.

6. Always remember, by this time tomorrow, thirty-five thousand Muslims will die without knowing Christ.

LEONARD ALBERT

Leonard Albert loves people in general and Muslims in particular. He has made nearly thirty trips to London, most recently witnessing to Muslims on the streets of London for ten days. A twenty-five-year career directing the ministry of laymen in the Church of God marks Leonard Albert as one of the evangelical church's most respected leaders in the field of lay ministries. He is a frequent guest speaker and seminar leader for national and international church gatherings, and his presentations are noted for his spiritual depth, knowledge of lay ministries, contagious enthusiasm, and delightful humor.

A native of Maine, Leonard earned a degree in Biblical Education from Lee University, Cleveland, Tennessee. He is the author of five books and manuals, including the popular Evangelism Breakthrough *and* Witnessing to the Cults. *Here is his advice for sharing Christ with a Muslim.*

About thirty years ago, I began to teach people how to share their faith in Christ in one-on-one encounters. I soon learned something that has stuck with me through the years: evangelism is more of a *process* than an *event.* For sure, there are times when we share the Gospel story or our personal testimony and we see immediate results. In this case we reap what I call a "John 4:38 experience" where the Bible says, *"Others have done the hard work, and you have reaped the benefits of their labor."* The thought is that if we win someone on the first encounter, someone else has probably been praying for and witnessing to the person for some time. We have come to realize that evangelism usually involves a process of time and takes a lot of prayer, persistence, and divine guidance.

The above is true as we share our faith with the followers of Mohammed. If you win a Muslim in the first encounter, either he or she wasn't a very good Muslim or someone else has already done the hard work and you were just there at the right time to reap the benefits.

Following Mohammed's death, Islam became an evangelistic movement. It quickly conquered North Africa, the Middle East, and central Asia. Islam is the only world religion that has ever dominated and taken over large populations and territories from the evangelical church world. A few years ago, I was privileged to travel to Turkey, a beautiful country that is 99 percent Muslim. All seven cities mentioned in the book of Revelation are in this country, and it is completely dominated by Islamic rule. Several areas where the Apostle Paul preached and planted churches are now under the crescent of Islam.

The Muslim world has been difficult to penetrate with the Gospel, but believers who are willing to prepare themselves can find a way to effectively share Christ. We will look at some "how to's" shortly, but as we begin, here are some general guidelines.

1. Show proper respect for human personality. If you examine the way Christ witnessed, you will soon realize that He always showed respect for the culture and the people to whom He communicated. He smashed the social taboos of the day by speaking to the woman at the well. He ministered at the other end of the spectrum by witnessing to Nicodemus, a powerful and wealthy member of the Sanhedrin. Everyone we meet, regardless of their social, cultural, or ethnic background, is worthy of our respect.

2. Learn to love the people of Islam. This is one trait that will get you through the most difficult encounters. A few months ago, I was invited to teach in a week-long conference on evangelism in London, England. The teaching sessions were scheduled in the morning, and each afternoon we went out on the streets and in the communities to meet people and share Christ. Since London is filled with Muslims, it was inevitable that we would encounter them as we ministered. That one week helped me to understand more about their culture than all the books I had previously read. *These people are serious about their faith!* It was a moving experience for me to be speaking to a Muslim for over an hour and hear him say with real conviction, "I pray to Allah that you would accept Mohammed as his prophet." These people are sincere! I did discover, however, that there are pious Muslims as well as lax ones, but the ratio of nominal people in Islam is lower than among Christians. Muslims cling tenaciously to their confessions of faith and repeat them daily. We have to realize that Christ died for them also, and He loves them with an everlasting love. We must show them the same

passion for our Bible as they have for their holy book, the Koran.

3. Have *knowledge* about their culture, beliefs, and practices. We must have a general working knowledge of Church history, the Koran, and some knowledge of the Muslim belief about Christ and Christianity. As we witness to them, we should know where they stand in their knowledge about evangelical Christianity. Here are just a few of the things they think about us and some of what they believe:

    a. They believe that Jews and Christians have deliberately distorted the Old and New Testaments to hide the predictions of the coming of Mohammed.

    b. They think we believe in three gods.

    c. They do not believe that it was Jesus who died on the cross. They believe another, such as Judas Iscariot, was crucified in His place.

    d. To them sin is the failure to live up to the Islamic moral code and the pillars of Islam.

    e. They fear hellfire.

    f. They believe there is a purgatory.

We must receive *empowerment* from Christ that will help us demonstrate the powerful gifts of healing, miracles, and signs and wonders. It is interesting to note that most Muslims will respect a visible, tangible, miraculous demonstration of the power of God. They are easily attracted to spiritual vitality. The truth is that they want to *see* it. Can the Christian community *show* it?

Those who anticipate interaction with Muslims must consider a method of approach. No other faith, not even

Judaism, is so resistant to the traditional "confrontational" or "encounter" approach that we find common in personal evangelism today. It will not be effective to just walk up to a Muslim and share the plan of salvation. Terms like *sin, salvation,* and *cross* that we commonly use in witnessing have an entirely different meaning for them. Since they deny that Jesus ever died on the cross, they simply cannot accept our understanding of salvation. Here are some simple steps that will help in our witnessing approach:

1. Establish *friendship.* The Muslim will be impressed with a Christian's words only if he experiences genuine friendship from the Christian and sees him living a consistently moral life. The goal is to demonstrate to these people the love and quality of life in Christ. It is better to win the Muslim as a friend than to win an argument and lose his friendship. Avoid critical remarks about Mohammed, the Koran, and Islam, even if your faith is criticized. Your patience, understanding, and display of friendship can cause the Muslim to be attracted to the Bible and to the Christian faith.

2. Pray for *discernment.* There will be times that only God can help you know what to say as you talk with Muslims.

3. Respect the *culture.* It will be easier if the Christian shares with his or her own gender if possible. Muslim men are very uncomfortable when approached by a woman as they are taught not to look a woman in the eyes for fear of temptation.

4. Seek *dialogue.* So much of our witnessing is monologue. We were created with two ears and one mouth—learn to use them accordingly! The best

evangelistic encounter with a Muslim is when there are plenty of questions asked from both sides. It is our job to listen, be attentive (be able to repeat back what is told to us), and ask plenty of questions so as to show respect and get them to open up and talk about their personal beliefs. A good way to open a dialogue is to ask a Muslim to tell you what his religion is and what he believes.

5. Find a witnessing *hook*. For me, it has been their respect for Moses the prophet and the acceptance of Christ as a prophet. There are four sacred writings in their religion: The books of Moses, the Psalms of David (Think of how we can use the wonderful prophecies concerning Christ from these Psalms!), the Gospels of Christ, and the Koran. They do feel that the Koran is the most accurate because it was the latest revelation. You've got to begin somewhere, and I think this is a great way to open up the discussion. Focus on the thought and question, "Who is Jesus?" Then begin to explore this concept in the Koran and in the Bible.

6. Share your *testimony*. Nothing will be more effective than for you to share the life-changing, life-transforming power of God in your life. Remember the Muslim mind is one of fatalism—they believe that whatever Allah wills will be and what is, is what Allah wills. Not so with our God! Through your testimony, you can relate the power of God to change the course of events and give you peace, real joy, and assurance of eternal life (three things that they do not have). Keep in mind that Muslims are very serious about visions and dreams. If you have had a genuine vision or dream from the Lord, don't be timid about sharing it, as it

can be the means of attracting that person to the Bible and Christianity.

7. Share the message of Christ. There is absolutely no substitute for the presentation of the Gospel. Have a care for the following high points of the Gospel.

a. *Share what God thinks of them.* The concept of God as a loving Heavenly Father is completely foreign to a Muslim. Show them from the Scriptures just how much God loves us . . . and them. Think of Jeremiah 31:3 where God says, *"I have loved you with an everlasting love."* Share the golden text of the Bible, John 3:16. It still works!

b. *Tell* them *the condition of man.* Explain the true meaning of sin in the sense that it is "missing the mark." It is a failure to live up to God's perfect standard as found in Matthew 5:48: *"Be perfect, therefore as your heavenly Father is perfect."* Show that we, as humans, cannot save ourselves. We need divine help.

c. *Show them God's plan for our freedom.* There is hope in Christ. We have to help them see that it was indeed Christ who died on the cross. But our hope is in the fact that He rose from the dead. The resurrection of Christ is the best way to show His power over sin. I recommend the book *More than a Carpenter* by Josh McDowell because it explains the deity of Christ in a simple, easy-to-understand style. We must show our friends that only through our blessed Savior can sins be forgiven. Show that God has provided a way whereby all sin can be forgiven and every trace of guilt can be completely removed.

d. *Help them make a commitment.* This is where you will learn that it takes time to win a Muslim convert. You have got to realize that in an Islamic society, there is no separation of church and state. The law of the Koran is the rule of all citizens, and to convert to another religion is an act of treason. Therefore, this will be a big step for a true Muslim believer. Explain that Christianity is not a religion but a relationship through Christ whereby we can know our Heavenly Father. The prospects must realize that Christ alone fills the void in their hearts and brings them into relationship with God.

8 Be *patient.* Remember we said it is a *process* and not an *event.* The Muslim has no cultural concept for the Gospel. For this reason, we should not become discouraged if there is no immediate response. Be patient with your Muslim friend. Continue to share the Gospel with prayer and faith, knowing that the Holy Spirit can make the truth real to them. Through the years of my teaching evangelism, I have always relied upon the powerful truth of John 16:8 that says, *"When he comes, he will convict the world of guilt in regard to sin and righteousness and judgment."* Our job is to share. It is the work of the Holy Spirit to convict and convince people of sin.

When a Muslim decides to follow Jesus Christ, this is really the beginning of our work. I think a key word here is "community." We have to rely on the body of Christ to come together and help disciple converts from Islam. The Church must be ready to receive and nurture them. Immediately, we must involve the person in a basic Bible study. We should be aware of the convert's family situation. He should be encouraged to discreetly witness to his family by sharing his new discoveries in the Bible. A visit to his home would be a good idea at this point. The goal is to make friends with his family. Also, at every opportunity we must pray with and for the new convert. And we must teach him to pray using the Lord's Prayer as a model. Lastly, we must encourage the new convert to become a part of a fellowship that will nurture their spiritual growth.

Most of the Muslims today claim a spiritual heritage from Ishmael. It is interesting to note that the name "Ishmael" is derived from the same root word as "Samuel" and means that "God hears" or "God answers." God has heard! He promised that He would make Ishmael a great nation. He has kept that promise! These people are part of God's plan for these last days. They are being won to Christ by the thousands! If we are not careful, we can slip into the false thinking that they will not respond to the Gospel and will not come to Christ. Such is not the case. Thousands of Muslims are becoming believers daily all over the world. May the power of the Holy Spirit cause us to have the initiative, the willingness, the knowledge, and the opportunity to share Christ with them wherever and whenever we meet them.

DAVID JOSEPH

Dr. David Joseph (his American name—not his birth name) was born in Egypt in 1955 and received Christ as his personal Savior 1972 in Cairo. He completed a degree in dentistry from Cairo University and was later elected the vice president of the Egyptian Medical Society. He later received a degree in journalism and became a magazine editor. In 1979, he founded a nonprofit Christian organization, "The Egyptian Christian Youth Union." It became the fastest growing interde-

nominational group in Egypt. In 1998, he planted a church for Middle Easterners in El Cajon, California, a suburb of San Diego. In 1999, he became professor of Islam and Middle East culture in Southern California Bible School and Seminary.

Dr. Joseph's vision is to teach believers how to reach Muslims and win them for Christ. Following are his tips on reaching Muslims with the Gospel.

The sole aim of this intensive look behind the veil is not to denounce Islam and Muslims but to educate Christian brothers and sisters, so they can effectively reach Muslims for Christ. It is also to help them warn those who have been deceived by Satan into accepting Islam as the true and Heavenly religion.

There are several things one must do to be able to win Muslims for Christ. Some of them include the following: Do not argue; pray and seek the Lord's guidance; have a knowledge of the Bible and the Koran; and demonstrate the love of the Holy Spirit toward Muslims.

Islam is not just a different way to worship God as many Western brothers and sisters think. It is not just a collection of teachings, theories, and doctrines. At its core is a spirit enticing Muslims to worship "Allah," who was a well-known pagan god before Islam began. Therefore, it is a spiritual battle, and Muslims cannot be won to Christ by arguments about theological issues. Although a Christian can win an argument if he is well versed in the teachings of the Bible and the Koran, he may lose his Muslim friend and drive him away from knowing Christ as his personal Savior.

When reaching out to Muslims, it's important to remember what the apostle Paul told the Corinthians, *"And my speech and my preaching were not with persuasive words of human wisdom, but in demonstration of the Spirit and of power"* (1 Corinthians 2:4 NKJV). Jesus taught us that people can come to Him only if they are drawn by God's Holy Spirit. (See John 6:44.)

Muslims believe that the Koran is perfect and contains all they need for life and eternity; they do not doubt its authenticity. Muslims believe Allah gave Mohammed the Koran word for word through the angel Gabriel, whom they believe to be the Holy Spirit.

It is very helpful to know how Muslims view the Koran. In the preface to the Koran of King Fahd Ibn Abdul Aziz Al-Saud (King of Saudi Arabia), the writer claimed that the Koran enjoys a number of unique characteristics. Three of these claims are listed below, followed by some questions to help you know whether the item is true.

1. It is the actual word of Allah, not created but revealed for the benefit of all mankind. It is stated in Sura Al-Furqan 1, "Blessed is He who sent down the Criterion to his servant (Mohammed) that it may be an admonition to all creatures."

    a. If the Koran is an admonition to all creatures, then why does it have to be written, recited, and used in all Muslim prayers in the Arabic language only?

    b. If it is for all creatures, why did Allah say, "Woe to anyone who asks for the meaning of these words"?

2. It is a theoretical and practical book, not only moralizing but also defining specifically the permissible and the forbidden. The importance of understanding the message of the Koran is undeniable, but simply reciting it with the intention of seeking Allah's pleasure and reward is also considered an act of worship

and meritorious in itself. Allah says, "So take what the Prophet gives you and refrain from what he prohibits you" (Sura Al Hashr 7).

   a. Is Allah pleased with forcing non-Arabs to recite the Koran in Arabic, as happens now in Sudan, and mandating that other non-Arabic countries learn the Koran only in Arabic? Is it an act of worship to chant verses from a "holy book" that you do not understand?

   b. Is the Koran a "practical book" when it asks husbands to scourge their wives?

3. Allah has perfected his religion for all mankind with the revelation of this book. He says, "This day have I perfected your religion for you, completed my favor upon you and have chosen for you Islam as your religion" (Sura Al Ma'ida 3).

   a. Did the Koran perfect religion for mankind, or does it cause confusion by mentioning things that the Bible does not mention and saying the opposite of what the Bible states in many cases (e.g., denying very essential facts, like the crucifixion of Christ)?

   b. Did God see the Koran as a favor to mankind by repeating the commands and rules of the Old Testament as if Jesus never came to the earth and as if the Holy Spirit never came to dwell in us?

We rejoice that God's Book (the Bible) has stood in the face of attempts to destroy it. It can speak for itself.

If the Koran has been revealed to the prophet Mohammed, how can we solve the well-known dilemma that Islam existed before Mohammed? Allah was already worshiped as a pagan idol, and certain tenets of Islam (such as fasting during Ramadan and worship at Al Kaaba—the black stone in Saudi Arabia) were in practice before Mohammed was born.

To reach Muslims for Christ, you and I have to do something. You may ask what do I have to offer them? Following are some ideas:

1. You must change your attitude toward Muslims. Many in the West consider Muslims to be trouble-makers, who refuse to receive Christ as their personal Savior. But this is not true of all Muslims. The majority long to know God and to have the assurance of going to Heaven. God placed those desires in the hearts of all mankind, but many are deceived by the teachings of Islam. The Holy Spirit can break the attitude that all Muslims are evil.

2. Remember the command of the Lord Jesus before He ascended into Heaven: *"Go into all the world and preach the Gospel to every creature"* (Mark 16:15 NKJV). God also had the Muslims in mind when Jesus gave us this command.

3. Muslims have many needs that you cannot provide because of the language, culture, and religious barriers between the West and the Middle East. But that does not mean that we should forget about them. You can support a missionary, church, or organization to meet these needs on your behalf.

The most urgent need is for Muslims to hear, read, and see the Word of God. We must offer them Bibles and Christian materials that are sensitive to their culture and are designed specifically for their understanding. We often use a vocabulary of "strange" Christian terminology when communicating the Gospel to them, such as:

"Dear brother, you have to know that *God, your Father, loves* you so much that He gave His only *Son* for you. He wants you to be *a believer* and to know Jesus as your *personal Savior.* He will give you a new nature instead of the *sinful nature you have.* If you want to *give your life to Jesus,* you can *pray now* and God will *guarantee your entrance into Heaven* to be with Him forever." It is a salvation message that Christians can understand, but for the Muslim there are many problems. For instance in the mind of a Muslim:

1. *"God your Father"* God cannot be some man or woman's father. God is the master and men are slaves. This is the only relationship between God and man that exists in Islam.

2. *"God loves you"* God also does not love mankind unconditionally. God loves only strong believers in Islam, the love of master to his good slave, not the father to his son. "God the Father" and "God is love" are two names missing among the most beautiful names of Allah in Islam.

3. *"His only Son"* God (Allah) has no son in Islam. When Christians say that Jesus is the Son of God, they think that God married the virgin Mary who conceived Jesus. So the Muslims will not accept the Christian belief that the Father and the Son are both God. Christians do not worship three Gods, and they do not accept that God had physical sex with Mary to create Jesus.

4. *"A believer"* A believer in Islam is one who recites what is called the two witnesses: "There is no god but Allah and Mohammed is the prophet of Allah." Reciting this sentence is enough to make a person a believer in Islam. Muslims believe they must recite a

"witness" to become a Christian, and they will not deny their Islamic witness.

5. *"Your personal Savior"* There is not "personal" relationship between man and Allah.

6. *"A new nature instead of the sinful nature"* Muslims will not understand what you are talking about. Islam does not teach that man has a sinful nature since the fall of Adam and Eve. Sins in Islam are specific acts, not a result of a sinful nature—so there is no need for salvation.

7. *"Give your life to Jesus"* Jesus is only a prophet of Allah in Islam. Some say that He died and Allah brought Him to Heaven. Some believe that God brought Him to Heaven and He still lives and will come again to die and return to Heaven. All Muslims believe that Jesus was never crucified, and, after all, He is a man like Adam and cannot give eternal life to anyone because it is only God's ability.

8. *"Pray with me now"* Prayer in Islam is not simply talking to Allah, because no one can do that. Prayer is a recitation. You cannot tell a Muslim that we will pray each of the five prayers he must do every day. For a Muslim to pray, he has to bow to the ground, look toward Mecca, and recite parts of the Koran for his prayer. Even if you are willing to pray like him, a Muslim cannot pray with you because you are not a Muslim.

9. *"Guarantee your entrance to Heaven to be with Him forever"* No one in Islam can guarantee that he will go to Heaven or be with Allah.

Muslims need to hear the Word of God. Christian radio programs are one of the most effective ways to reach

Muslims. Although Christian television in the Middle East is more effective, Arabic-speaking pastors are afraid to appear on them for fear of the government. Thank God for The Voice of the Martyrs and their help to win Muslims for Christ and to help the suffering Church in the Islamic world.

Not all Muslims think exactly alike. As we witness to Muslims, we need guidance from the Holy Spirit to discern the following.

Find out what your Muslim friend thinks of Christianity.

Each Muslim has a different reaction to the Gospel as a whole. These reactions have been categorized into seven areas, as follows:

1. A Muslim who does not like to discuss any social or religious topic with a Christian so as not to defile himself. A believer cannot communicate with this kind of Muslim except through his lifestyle and character, being a good example of a Christian. Jesus said, *"Let your light shine before men, that they may see your good deeds and praise your Father in Heaven"* (Matthew 5:16). The Muslims must see something different in the Christian that sets him apart from others.

2. A Muslim who has a positive attitude toward Christians but does not like to discuss religion. This kind of person also needs to see Christians live out their faith, but he is more open to listen when they talk about social issues that lead to discussion on religion.

3. A Muslim who can talk about religion but who attacks the Bible and doctrinal issues. His intent is to force Islam on the Christian. He firmly believes in the divine origin of Islam. This kind of Muslim needs someone to listen to him until he finishes. Always

answer his questions with a question. For example, the Muslim may ask: "Do you believe that the Bible you read is the same one that was inspired by God?"

Christian: Yes, I do; what do you believe?

Muslim: This is not the original Bible; it is a corrupt one.

Christian: Do you know where I can find a copy of the original?

Muslim: No, I do not, but I am sure that this one is a corrupt Bible.

Christian: Can you tell me when that happened? Did the corruption occur before or after Islam?

Muslim: Before Islam, of course.

Christian: Then why did the prophet of Islam ask the people of the Book, the Christians and the Jews, to observe the Torah and the Injil (the Old and New Testaments), asking them to view them as a reference and as valid books? Sura 5:68 in the Koran says, " O people of the book! Ye have no ground to stand upon unless ye stand fast by the Torah, the Gospel, and all the revelation that has come to you from your Lord. It is the revelation that cometh to thee from the Lord." According to Sura 10:94, Allah also told Mohammed that if he had doubts about anything being revealed to him, he may ask the people of the book. "If you doubt what we have revealed to you, ask those who have read the Scriptures before you. The truth has come to you from your Lord: therefore do not doubt, nor shall you deny the revelations of God, for then you shall be lost."

Continue to answer your Muslim friend using questions that help him to think about the answers, moving him toward the Truth. This is one of the most important things we can do when witnessing.

4. A Muslim who is open to hearing what you have to say without any arguments; he just wants to hear, not respond. This kind of Muslim needs a very simple Christian message. As you ask him questions, do not expect him to answer or react to them. You may say, "What is meant by redemption?" Then you answer, "Redemption means that an innocent person has to die for the guilty one. Who is the most suitable one for that? Of course, Jesus is the only One."

5. A Muslim who is open to the truth of Christianity is ready to discuss your questions and is faithful in respecting you and the Bible. This kind of Muslim needs someone who can answer all of his questions. Most Muslims who fit this description are usually convinced with your message.

6. A Muslim who has doubts about Islam and asks questions about Christianity. A person well-versed in Islam is needed to answer his questions about either Islam or Christianity, making comparisons between the two.

7. A Muslim who loves Christ and asks how he can accept Jesus as his personal Savior needs the simple Gospel message and encouragement to express his feelings to God at this point.

There are two more things about which we need to pray and seek guidance of the Lord, so we can understand our Muslim brothers and sisters and be able to reach them effectively: 1) *To know the real needs of the Muslim.* (Does he fear the Day of Judgment and eternity? Does he need forgiveness?) and 2) *To know the right time to talk with the Muslim.* If you know what your Muslim friend thinks of Christianity, the Holy Spirit will give you guidance to know the right time to share the Gospel. Remember, Jesus said, *"No one can come to me unless the Father who sent me draws him"* (John 6:44).

One of the most important points in sharing the Gospel with Muslims is to know the teachings of both the Bible and the Koran. You must know what each book says about the subjects you are discussing, such as sin, salvation, God's love, the way to Heaven, eternal life, Hell, assurance of salvation, who intercedes on our behalf, etc.

The answers to these questions in the Koran are completely different from those found in the Bible. Islam teaches that sin is simply an action and that man does not have a sinful nature. Therefore, there is nothing to be saved from. One just needs to repent and do good deeds, and sins are forgiven.

Islam also teaches that no one can enter Heaven. Heaven is the throne of God, and God has no personal relationship with mankind. The Garden, or Paradise, is the place where man goes. The only way to get to Paradise is to do good deeds, pray, fast, give alms to the poor, visit Mecca (the birthplace of Islam) if possible, and recite the Islamic creed ("There is no God but Allah and Mohammed is the Messenger of Allah").

Even with all that, there is no guarantee that one will go to Paradise. It is up to Allah whether he allows someone into Paradise or Hell. Muslims also believe that Mohammed, the prophet of Islam, is the only one from whom Allah will accept intercession. He can intercede on someone's behalf, even after that person's death.

To reach Muslims, you must know the questions most frequently asked by Muslims and know the biblical answers. Following is sample dialogue for questions Muslims may ask:

Q. Do you believe that God is one person or more than one?

A. Christians believe that God has three parts but is only one God, as stated in the Bible. (Show him 1 John 5:7-8; it will be more efficient if you let the Muslim friend read it for themselves.)

Q. Do you believe that the Bible is the same as the original one and that no one has corrupted it? You cannot prove anything from a corrupted book.

A. The Bible is not corrupted and my proofs are as follows . . . (This is why Christians need to understand their own faith very well.)

Q. Then who is Jesus?

A. He is the Word of God, as stated in the Bible in John 1:1-2 and even in the Koran in Sura 3:45. He is the Spirit of God (Sura 4:171). He is a messenger of God (Sura 4:171).

Q. Is Jesus the Son of God?

A. Yes, He is (Romans 1:3-4).

Q. Did God marry and father a son?

A. No. (Explain to him the meaning of Son of God, that Jesus is God incarnate.)

Q. Does God eat, drink, and go to the restroom?

A. There is a difference between the body of Jesus and the Spirit of God. In the Koran, God has all the characteristics of man; for example God has a face, He can see, talk, love, hate, sit, stand, etc., so it is not strange that God who has these characters in the Koran can reveal Himself as a man in Jesus Christ.

Q. Does the New Testament abolish the Old Testament and the Koran abolish the Injil?

A. God will never change His Word. If God is all knowing, He does not need to give an order and then change it, since He knows every single thing from the beginning to the end.

Q. Would you give me an example?

A. When God ordered the Jews to leave Egypt, they were small in number and faced many great nations. But God told them to not be afraid of them and to not accept their idols and worship them but destroy them. When they became well armed, He told them the same thing. He never abolished what He told them from the beginning, because He wanted to teach them that the victory is from the Lord and it will never depend upon their power or number. Allah did not do the same when Muslims were few in number. Allah initially did not ask them to fight the Christians or the Jews but gave Mohammed the "nicest" Suras about both Christians and Jews. When Mohammed had a large army, Allah abolished the nice way of dealing with Christians and Jews and replaced it with a very hard way.

Q. Do you think that the Koran and the Bible have the same origin?

A. Of course not, since they contain completely different and contradictory teachings. I really know the Bible is from God.

Most important is to practice the love of the Holy Spirit with the Muslims. Without loving them, you will never be able to win them for Christ. The message that you share with the Muslims must be the message of Jesus Christ, not that he must leave his religion and become a Christian. Explain that by accepting Jesus as his personal Savior, he can escape the punishment of Hell and have eternal life.

TAYSIR ABU SAADA

Taysir Abu Saada, who goes by "Tass," is a former Palestinian freedom fighter. Over the years he struck up a friendship with successful businessman Charles Sharpe. One day, Tass noticed some changes in Charlie that he could not explain. He found out that Charlie had received Christ. Years passed. Finally one day in conversation, Charlie challenged Tass that he did not "fear God." This was offensive to Tass, as a Muslim, to be told that he did not fear God. But Charlie continued, "and you need to love Jewish people." This was more than Tass could conceive. How could he love the people he once hated? Tass's hunger intensified. Finally Charlie decided to read the gospel of John to Tass. As Tass reports it, something hit him. He began to shake. He actually blacked out. He awakened on the floor, feeling as if something was lifting him off the floor. And this dramatic and unusual moment proved to be a life-changing conversion. The evidence is in the "fruit": his deep love for Jews (whom he previously hated) and for Muslims (which he used to be). Tass's witnessing style, as you soon shall see, is simple: love them.

I have found that at the basis of every successful witness is a good relationship between the Muslim and Christian. Also, a few other things need to be taken into consideration such as the culture. Muslims come from a wide variety of cultures, and these differences in culture play key roles in our understanding and our approach in witnessing.

In the past, American Christians have not been subjected to the kind of fear Islam strikes in the hearts and memories of the Church worldwide. This fear has its genesis several centuries ago when Eastern nations were subjugated by the sword of Islam's might. Under some of the rulers, they suffered injustices and despotic treatment, which left deep-seated fear in people's minds. Such is the case with every subjugated nation whose rights have been violated. It is my opinion that with the recent attacks on U.S. soil by "so-called" zealots of the Islamic faith, America has experienced (like it or not) a "sword of Islam."

Because of this, I have come to understand how intimidated Christians are by Muslims. This is true for Arab Christians as well. I believe the reason for this is the fact that Christians have been ignorant of Islam and its Muslim followers. Thus, Christians have sometimes attacked Islam (demeaning remarks regarding Hagar and Ishmael) without fully understanding Muslims.

In studying the Islamic religion, one will be amazed to discover the noble qualities and profound moral teachings contained in their books. My findings suggest that the Church is in need of leaders aware of the essence of Islam. I would urge every worker in the Lord's field to give the Muslim question its fair share of study. Muslims have qualities to be admired for; they are not ashamed to show their religion and never cease from calling others to embrace it.

Before we discuss ways that enable us to reach Muslims, we have to understand how to approach them and to explain our purpose to them. We must realize that God has called us to preach the Gospel to every nation, including the Muslim nations. He has left to us the duty to believe and demonstrate the strength of our faith by sincerity of heart and purity of our purpose, which will bring about signs and wonders. Only through the supernatural love (Christ's love) and the strength of our witness (Holy Spirit-generated faith) can we hope to reach Muslims for Christ. *"Then the disciples went out and preached everywhere, and the Lord worked with them and confirmed his word by the signs that accompanied it"* (Mark 16:20).

We must ask ourselves, do we love them enough to devote our time to prayer and fasting, studying, and understanding them? We must begin there. If we are unwilling to enter into that basic commitment of ourselves, we will not succeed.

We must offer the Gospel to them "on the plate" of Christian love which never fails. It is with love alone that you will be able to gain their confidence and thus open the door to speak to them about their eternal life. How do I love them? Make sure you are lovable by their estimation by behaving according to God's Word: *"For this very reason, make every effort to add to your faith goodness; and to goodness, knowledge; and to knowledge, self-control; and to self-control, perseverance; and to perseverance, godliness; and to godliness, brotherly kindness; and to brotherly kindness, love"* (2 Peter 1:5-7).

If a Muslim is having difficulties, help them by trying to understand and realize the basis of their faith. They are trying their best but, like all people are tempted by evil. If you love them genuinely, you need to try to understand their feelings, and to do that, it is essential to study their beliefs closely, not seeking to find defects but understanding better those who hold these beliefs.

In approaching a Muslim, keep in mind not to come to them with speech that is unintelligible or strange to their ears. Use the Word of God, which has many verses that are easy to understand. Present them with proofs of the accuracy of the Bible and its freedom from alteration.

Never attack personalities respected by the Muslims, directly or indirectly. Always treat them with the kindness and patience of Christ so that the atmosphere will be one of confidence.

Gain knowledge of their customs, so you will know their customs and know how to help them accept the Gospel of salvation.

And, above all else, love them dearly with a pure heart so they will be assured of your good intentions and believe in the integrity and geniuneness of your witness.

You must realize that Muslims have been reared in a society that loves debate on major issues. However, rarely if ever does a Muslim accept the truth of the Gospel by argument.

Most Christians believe that it is not possible for a Muslim to receive the message of salvation sincerely. I (Taysir Abu Saada) am living proof that this is an erroneous belief.

Despite its complexity, the situation in the Middle East and its solution is vital to the peace of the entire world. That is why it is the duty of all Christians to seek after Muslim souls.

If God can turn me from being a terrorist to a peace-loving man, then I believe it is possible and that there is hope for all Muslims.

AUTHOR'S FINAL COMMENTS:

And with Taysir's optimistic words I close: *There is hope for all Muslims.*

ENDNOTES

1   Benjamin Netanyahu, "Statement of former Israeli Prime Minister Netanyahu before the Government Reform Committee, September 20, 2001," Committee on Government, Web page, Accessed: 1/10/02 (Washington, DC, Web address: *http://www.house.gov/reform/statement_of_netanyahu.htm*).

2   George Braswell, *What You Need to Know about Islam and Muslims* (Broadman & Holman, 2000), pp. 1-2.

3   Samuel P. Huntingdon, *The Clash of Civilizations and the Remaking of World Order* (Touchstone, 1996), pp. 110-119.

4   "Sharing Christ with Muslims," *Frontiers,* (no publisher, n.d.), p. 4.

5   Benjamin Netanyahu, "Statement."

6   Anis A. Shorrosh, *Islam Revealed* (Thomas Nelson Publishers, 1988), p. 54.

7   Ibid., p. 56.

8   George Braswell, *What You Need to Know about Islam and Muslims,* p. 13.

9   Anis A. Shorrosh, *Islam Revealed,* p. 59.

10 Ibid.

11 George Braswell, *What You Need to Know about Islam and Muslims,* p. 38.

12 "Sharing Christ with Muslims," *Frontiers,* p. 5; and also J. Dudley Woodberry, "Current Trends in Islam," (Lecture; Fuller Theological Seminary, December 10-14, 2001).

13 Anis A. Shorrosh, *Islam Revealed,* p. 26.

14 Kenneth J. Thomas, "Allah in Translations of the Bible," *The Bible Translator* 52:3, July, 2001; pp. 301-2.

15 Ibid., p. 301.
    Note: He is citing G. J. O. Moshay, *Who Is This Allah?*

16 George Braswell, *What You Need to Know about Islam and Muslims,* p. 22

17 John Obert Voll, *Islam, Continuity and Change in the Modern World* (Boulder, CO: Westview Press, 1982), p. 4.

18 Dr. J. Dudley Woodberry, "Current Trends in Islam," December 13, 2001.

19 Robert Morey, *The Islamic Invasion* (Harvest House, 1992), p. 20.

20 George Braswell, *What You Need to Know about Islam and Muslims,* p. 3.

21 Ernest Hahn, *How to Respond—Muslims* (St. Louis: Concordia Publishing House, 1995), p. 29.

[22] "Muslim Mosques Growing at a Rapid Pace in the U.S.," Hartford Institute for Religious Research. Web page (Hartford Seminary, Hartford CT: Last updated: 12/19/2001), Web site: *http://fact.hartsem.edu/Press/mediaadvsry5.htm.*

[23] Samuel P. Huntington, *The Clash of Civilizations and the Remaking of World Order,* p. 115.

[24] Note: Charles Colson's *Breakpoint* (Radio commentary #011214, December 14, 2001 is one of many such reports of Muslim violence against Christians in Indonesia).

[25] *MSNBC Special News Report,* (January 1, 2002).

[26] Ari and Shira Sorko-Ram, "What the Free World Doesn't Know about Terrorism," *Maoz Israel Report* (October 2001), p. 1.

[27] Moshe Feiglin "Why America Has Already Lost the War," Web site: Web page: *www.manhigut.org/english/articles-e/feiglin48-e.html* (September 28, 2001).

[28] "Graham Stands by Characterization of Islam as 'Wicked,'" *Cybercast News Service* (Sunday, November 18, 2001).

[29] Franklin Graham, "My View of Islam," *WSJ The Wall Street Journal Online.com, Opinion Journal,* December 9, 2001.

[30] George Braswell, *What You Need to Know about Islam and Muslims,* p. 87.

[31] Ibid, p. 4.

[32] Dr. J. Dudley Woodberry, "Current Trends in Islam," December 14, 2001).

[33] Samar Hathout, vice-chairperson of the Muslim Public Affairs Council in Los Angeles, "Challenges and Opportunities Facing American Muslim Women," Speech. United Nations Fourth World Conference on Women, Huairou, China (September 7, 1995; *zawaj.com,* reprinted from *Karamah.org).*

[34] James Beverley, "Is Islam a Religion of Peace?" *Christianity Today,* 46:1, January 7, 2002; p. 41.

[35] "The Omar Covenant", *Faqeeh Al-Muluk,* Volume 2, pp. 124-136.

[36] Abd El Schafi, *Behind the Veil,* 3rd printing (Caney, KS: Pioneer Book Company, 2001), pp. 7-8.

[37] James A. Beverley "Is Islam a Religion of Peace?" p. 40
Note: The article cites a portion of Beverley's book entitled *Understanding Islam,* (Thomas Nelson Publishers, 2002).

[38] Ibid.

[39] See Charles Kurzman, editor, *Liberal Islam, A Sourcebook* (New York: Oxford University Press, 1998).

[40] Dr. J. Dudley Woodberry, "Current Trends in Islam," Chart. (Fuller Seminary, Pasadena, CA, Dec. 2001).

[41] "California Pupils Indoctrinated in Islam," *NewsMax.com,* America's News Page. Web page, Accessed: 1/17/02. Web Address: *http://www.newsmax.com/showinside.shtml?a=2002/1.*

[42] Ray Waddle, "Some Churches Becoming Places to Learn about Islam," *Tennessean.com.* Website: *www.tennessean.com* (Tuesday, October 16, 2001, Nashville: *The Tennessean).*
Note: No longer available online.

[43] Note: For a good analysis of this event see Tom White, "Have We Shamed the Face of Jesus? Muslims in Our Pulpits," *The Voice of the Martyrs Ministry Letter,* Bartlesville, OK (undated letter, received December 2001), pp. 1-2.
Note: Tom White's letter can also be found on the following Web page: *http://www.persecution.com/editorial/index.cfm?editorialID=10.*

[44] Note: Although Crusaders committed atrocities, the Crusades were waged for the purpose of defending or recovering lands and peoples threatened by Moslem aggressors.

[45] Note: In one case, the pastor of Trinity Lutheran Church in Lebanon, MO, the Rev. David Oberdieck, filed church charges with the Lutheran Church-Missouri Synod over a fellow pastor who joined non-Christian clergy in the September 23 Yankee Stadium service, "A Prayer for America (Associated Press, *The Washington Times,* Web site: *http://www.washtimes.com/national/20011202-75389440.htm).*

[46] American Religious Identification Survey (ARIS), (The Graduate Center at the City University of New York, 2001) reported by *Charisma News Service,* 3:194, Friday, December 28, 2001.

[47] *World Magazine,* 16:46, December 1, 2001.

[48] Dr. Graham Walker, phone interview, (Thursday, September 13, 2001).

[49] Capitol Hill Prayer Alert Foundation E-mail, [Friday, December 7, 2001].

[50] Dave Clarke, "Free Abortions Offered in NYC," *www.family.org, A Web site of Focus on the Family: Family Issues in Policy and Culture.* Web page: *http://www.family.org/cforum/fnif/news/a0017962.html* (October 5, 2001).

[51] Elwood McQuaid, "Who Weeps for Hagar's Children?" *Israel My Glory Magazine* 59:6, November/December 2001; p. 6.

POTENTIAL READING

Alphabetized by author's last name (or book title where no author is listed)

30 Days Muslim Prayer Focus. Tenth-Anniversary Edition (November 17 to December 16, 2001). Colorado Springs: World Christians News and Books, 2001.

This is a prayer journal guiding Christians to pray for Muslims during their holy month of Ramadan. New and updated each year, it is superbly written and highly informative. It takes only minutes daily as a devotional thought. A "must" for every Christian who desires to get a glimpse of what God wants to do among Muslims. This book helps provide one with a compassionate prayer life for Muslims

Accad, Fouad Elias. *Building Bridges: Christianity and Islam*. Colorado Springs: NavPress, 1997.

This book is the account of Pastor Accad, who died in 1994, who dedicated his life to reconciliation between Christians and Muslims. Although it is an outstanding book in demonstrating love for Muslims, it "stretches" certain issues (such as contending that the Koran supports the crucifixion of Jesus).

Arise Shine Morocco, 52 Weeks of Prayer for Morocco & Its Peoples. No location listed: ASM (Arise ShineMorocco), n.d.

The booklet lists only *www.interim.org/ASM* as the source for information.

This is a superb prayer journal, designed to last for an entire year, focusing on a country that often ranks in the "top ten" worst persecutors of Christians. While no author is listed, the book is superb as a prayer guide. More books like this will be needed in order for Christians to be able to pray in an informed way regarding Islamic nations.

Armstrong, Karen. *Islam, a Short History*. New York: The Modern Library, 2000.

Armstrong is a freelance writer and broadcaster in London. Formerly professor of Modern Literature, London University. She is a visiting faculty member of the Center for Muslim-Christian Understanding, Georgetown University. Armstrong's writing style makes this a very readable book. But she excuses every violent act committed by Muslims, blaming "the West" (the U.S.) for Islamic violence—right down to the final paragraph. The book loses credibility due to its *rabid* pro-Islam (almost a "Muslims can do no wrong") bias. In spite of the obvious lack of objectivity and the harpooning of everything Western, the chronology in the front pages and the appendixes make this worth purchasing.

Author's note: Although I personally disagree with much of this book, I learned years ago that "conservatives" are sufficiently intellectually "secure" to read the writings of "liberals." Academic and political liberals do not demonstrate that same "security," and therefore, as a condescending act, rarely mention or read books by so-called "conservatives."

Beverley, James A. *Understanding Islam.* Nashville: Thomas Nelson, 2001. This book was published after September 11, 2001.

This book is a type of primer and is part of a series in Thomas Nelson's *Quick Guides* to religions. At less than ninety pages it is easy reading; it reads like *U.S.A. Today.* It is succint and user friendly. Beverly is an expert on world religions and a professor at Tyndale Seminary in Toronto.

Braswell, George. *What You Need to Know about Islam and Muslims.* Nashville: Broadman & Holman, 2000.

Braswell uses a "clinical" writing style. He is dispassionate, but tremendously informative. If you can only read one book on the topic, get this one.

Buchanan, Patrick. *The Death of the West: How Mass Immigration, Depopulation and a Dying Faith Are Killing Our Culture and Country.* New York: St. Martin's Press, 2001.

Highly controversial, as usual. But analytically skilled, as usual. Buchanan takes present immigration and population "shift" statistics and projects what will occur by 2050. Its relevance for our purposes is the predicted Islamic "takeover" of Europe. The "politically correct" crowd will disdain this work. Read it and make up your own mind.

Dowley,Tim. *The Baker Atlas of Christian History.* Grand Rapids: Baker Books, 1997.

This is a spectacular atlas with 160 full color maps, tracing the growth of Christianity in a way that anyone can understand. So why include it in a book about Islam? Because some of the maps show Islam's staggering growth (pp. 87-8, 98-9). Very enlightening book. The visuals are invaluable. Put it on this year's Christmas wish list. It's worth it.

Esposito, John L. *The Islamic Threat, Myth or Reality?* New York: Oxford University Press, 1999.

Esposito, director of the Center for Muslim-Christian Understanding at Georgetown University, was a consultant to the State Department during the Carter years. The book is academic in focus. It requires an enormous amount of time to read. Esposito cannot say a negative word about Islam, contending that critics of Islam have failed to distinguish between the legitimate use of force in self-defense and terrorism (p. 286). This book would likely be unsettling to the Christians around the world that are persecuted by Muslims.

Geisler, Norman L. & Abdul Saleeb. *Answering Islam: The Crescent in Light of the Cross.* Baker Book House, 1993.

Geisler is the president of Southern Evangelical Seminary in Charlotte, NC, and is the author or editor of nearly 40 books. He is a leading Christian apologist. This is a technical book, but anything by Geisler, buy it. Well researched. Extremely helpful. Ranks high in the "Top Ten" books you need on the topic.

The Hadith, (I used the following on-line resource) *http://db.islam.org:81/hadith/ssearch.htm.*

Hahn, Ernest. *How to Respond—Muslims.* St. Louis: Concordia Publishing House, 1995.

Simple. Readable. Digestible. Helpful.

Huntington, Samuel P. *The Clash of Civilizations and the Remaking of World Order.* New York: Touchstone, Simon & Schuster, 1996.

Huntingdon, a Harvard University professor, was director of security planning for the National Security Council in the Carter administration. The sections on Islam are "must" reading. Provocative. Enlightening.

Jomier,Jacques. *How to Understand Islam.* New York: Crossroad Publishing Company, 1999.

This is a superb book written from a Catholic perspective. Jomier notes that he does not want to focus on the "negative," thus he largely omits from the story the severe treatment of Christians by Muslims. However, this book is highly informative, easily read. This one makes the "Top Five" list.

Khalil, Victor. *The Truth of the Quran in the Light of the Bible.* Seventh edition. (self-published), 1999.

Written by Egyptian Victor Khalil, this book attempts to lovingly lead Muslims to Christ.

_____. *To You, My Lady.* Colorado Springs: Al-Nour, n.d.
Khalil views women as the key to setting Muslims free to the
Gospel of Jesus Christ.

Koran, The (The Qu'ran).
For personal study, I used two different translations: *The Qu'ran,*
translated by M. H.Shakir, Elmhurst, New York: Tahrike Tarsile
Qur'an, Eighth U.S. Edition, 1999 and *The Koran,* translated by N.
J. Dawood, Penguin Books, 2000.

The preferred translation is: *The Holy Qur'an: Text, Translation, and
Commentary,* Abdallah Yusuf Ali. New Revised Edition. Brentwood,
MD: Amana Corporation, 1989.

For on-line research, I used: *http://www.stg.brown.edu/webs/
quran_browser/pqeasy.shtml.* (Note: Versification [numbering of
verses] may vary from one translation to the next.)

Kurzman, Charles, editor. *Liberal Islam, a Sourcebook.* New York:
Oxford University Press, 1998.
Kurzman, professor at University of North Carolina at Chapel Hill,
contends that in addition to "customary Islam" and "revivalist Islam
(Islamism, fundamentalism)" there is a third group: "liberal Islam"
which describes Muslims attempting to come to grips with moder-
nity. Purely academic. Slow reading. But a good balance for those
who are never exposed to anything but fundamentalist Islam.

Love, Fran and Jeleta Eckheart, editors. *Ministry to Muslim Women,
Longing to Call Them Sisters.* Pasadena: William Carey Library,
2000.
Edited compilations from the Consultation on Ministry to Muslim
Women, a conference taking place in Mesa, Arizonia, in 1999.
Written by women—for women.

Martinson, Paul Varo, editor. *Islam: An Introduction for Christians.*
Minneapolis: Augsburg, 1994.
First published in German, this book is helpful in understanding
Christian-Muslim relations. It is weak in acknowledging the violent,
fundamentalist components of Islam and is seemingly blind to the
persecution of Christians in Islamic nations. The superbly helpful
appendixes make the book worth its price. (It comes with an
accompanying booklet: Irene R. Getz, *Islam: An Introduction for
Christians, Leader's Guide,* Minneapolis: Augsburg, 1994.)

McCurry, Don. *Healing the Broken Family of Abraham: New Life for
Muslims.* Colorado Springs: Ministries to Muslims, 2001.

This book is superb—a must reading for anyone wanting to reach out to Muslims. McCurry shows tremendous grasp of the complexity of ministry to the various "strands" of Islam. This one definitely makes it into the "Top Ten."

Morey, Robert. *The Islamic Invasion*. Eugene, OR: Harvest House Publishers, 1992.
The content is superior to the writing style. Whereas Braswell (mentioned above) is dispassionate, Morey is visceral. He "goes for the jugular." Morey is a vigorous debater, and it shows in the writing style. It is definitely worth reading. Particularly, read the appendixes regarding the Hadith. If you can only read two books on the topic, make this one of them.

Nazir-Ali, Michael. *Islam: A Christian Perspective*. Philadelphia: Westminster Press, 1983.
Though it has a lot of content, it is bulky and cumbersome in style. It is not user-friendly and is too academic for most readers.

Renard, John. *Responses to 101 Questions on ISLAM*. New York: Paulist Press, 1998.
The book, while providing some helpful historical data, is so blatantly pro-Muslim that it fails any test of objectivity. It advocates "Islam is a religion of peace" throughout. This does not help persons understand the persecution of Christians and Jews that has occurred for centuries. It is a disappointing book with a catchy title.

Rippin, Andrew, Muslims, *Their Beliefs and Practices, Volume 1: The Formative Period*, London: Routledge, 1990.
This work reads like a doctoral dissertation, so it is excellent for academicians—far too "bulky" for others.

Saal, William J. *Reaching Muslims for Christ*. Chicago: Moody Press, 1991.
Saal's book contains a lot of information. It is well written and easy to grasp. It is helpful for those serious about evangelizing Muslims.

Sadik, Nasr, *A Quran from Allah?* self-published, Second edition, 1998.
Designed to help Muslims enter into intellectual honesty and spiritual freedom.

Schafi, Abd El. *Behind the Veil*. Third edition. Caney, KS: Pioneer Book Company, 2001.
Although Caney's book is a bit technical, it is extremely helpful. He explains Islamic law, tracing historic Muslim scholars on many contemporary topics. I highly recommend it.

Sharing Christ with Muslims. Booklet. United Kingdom: Frontiers Missions, n.d.

This is a superb, quick overview of Islam. It only takes a few minutes to read.

Shorrosh, Anis A. *Islam Revealed, a Christian Arab's View of Islam.* Nashville: Thomas Nelson, 1988.

Shorrosh, a Christian evangelist, has publicly debated some of Islam's best-known defenders. If you have time to read only three books on the topic, make sure this is one of them, since it is easily read and profoundly informative. It functions as a superb "primer."

Smith, Jane I. *Islam in America.* New York: Columbia University Press, 1999.

Smith's book is clearly an academic book, but very easy reading and superbly written. She gives the reader a unique look at Islam's growing presence and influence in America. Smith is professor of Islamic Studies at Hartford Seminary in Connecticut. The underlying "theme" seems to be that Muslims are very often stereotyped and misunderstood. Islam's "darker side" is never discussed in books of this type.

Tanagho, Samy. *Glad News! God Loves You My Muslim Friend.* Santa Ana: Good Shepherd World Evangelism, 2001.

Tanagho studied Islam Law at The Ain Shams University of Law, Cairo, Egypt, and was a practicing attorney. This book is practical, helpful, and easily understood. A superb Christian apologetic designed exclusively for Muslims.

Voll, John Obert. *Islam, Continuity and Change in the Modern World,* Boulder, CO: Westview Press, 1982. (Note: was updated by Syracuse University Press, 1994.)

This is a highly academic book. Voll is affiliated with the Center for Muslim-Christian Understanding, Georgetown University. His work is laborious to read. However, it is well worth it to the serious student of Islam, since it traces the complex historical roots of the many "strains" of Islam.

Woodberry, J. Dudley. "Current Trends in Islam." MR 556, 124-page class syllabus, Fuller Theological Seminary, Pasadena, CA 91182, Winter, 2002.

Admittedly this might not be readily available, but if the Fuller Seminary bookstore will sell it, buy it. Full of insightful glimpses of contemporary Islam. Dr. Woodberry, who received his Ph.D. in Islamic Studies at Harvard, has divided the last fifty years between the Middle East and Fuller Seminary. He is the consummate gentleman (he will not *debate* Muslims, insisting on respectful *dialogue* with Muslims), in contrast to Robert Morey (listed above) who is the passionate "I-dare-you" debater of Muslims. It takes all kinds! Woodberry has been a guest lecturer in nearly thirty-five Muslim nations.

Ye'or, Bat, *The Decline of Eastern Christianity under Islam, from Jihad to Dhimmitude,* Madison: Fairleigh Dickinson University Press, 1996. Ye'or coined the word "dhimmitude" to study non-Muslims living under the Islamic law—the shari'a. In a review of the book, William Montgomery Watt stated that the book raises the question, "Does the *shari'ah* allow Muslims to live peaceably with non-Muslims in the 'one world?'" Breathtaking, yet intimidating book. Academic in style. Allow a very long time to read it.

Zebiri, Kate. *Muslims and Christians Face to Face.* Oxford: One World, 1997. Admittedly designed for graduate courses. This book is not casual reading, though quite interesting. Zebiri traces Christian and Muslim literature—what they are saying about each other—from academic to "popular."

ADDITIONAL RESOURCES

Beverley, James A. "The Best Resources on Islam," *Christianity Today.* Jan. 7, 2002, Volume 46, Number 1, p. 36. This is an excellent listing of resources on Islam.

SEPTEMBER 11 BOOKS

Pastors and Christian Authors Responding to September 11, 2001:

Cymbala, Jim, *God's Grace from Ground Zero*
Hagee, John, *Attack on America*
Hayford, Jack, *How to Live through a Bad Day*
Lucado, Max, *America Looks Up*
MacArthur, John, *Terrorism, Jihad and the Bible*
Stanley, Charles, *When Tragedy Strikes*
Swindoll, Charles R., *Why, God?*
Tenney, Tommy, *Trust and Tragedy*

For more information from the author, see *www.jimgarlow.com.*